ADVANCING I

M000296296

ADVANCING INNOVATION

*Galvanizing, Enabling & Measuring
for Innovation Value!*

Patrick J. Stroh, CMA

The Association of
Accountants and
Financial Professionals
in Business

Advancing Innovation
Galvanizing, Enabling, & Measuring For Innovation Value

Cover Image: Jay Highum, Action Graphic Designs
Cover Design: Exeter Premedia Services

Institute of Management Accountants
10 Paragon Drive, Suite 1
Montvale, NJ 07645

www.imanet.org

Because of the dynamic nature of the Internet, any Web addresses or
links contained in this book may have changed since publication and
may no longer be valid. The views expressed in this work are solely
those of the author and do not necessarily reflect the views of the
publisher, and the publisher hereby disclaims any responsibility for them.

ISBN: 978-0-9967293-07(sc)
ISBN: 978-0-9967293-14(ebk)

First Edition

Praise for *Advancing Innovation*

"Advancing Innovation does a fantastic job of wrapping a strategic lens around innovation and linking it to solid governance. (It) plants the seeds to help decision makers get a grip on how innovation takes shape, feeds into strategy and, ultimately, value creation."

—Sandra B. Richtermeyer, Ph.D., CMA, CPA, Associate Dean, Williams College of Business, Xavier University

"As someone actively working with business leaders to define and solve their business problems for the past 35 years, what I like most about Patrick Stroh's book, *Advancing Innovation*, is its focus on linking innovation to value creation. This is not just a book of traditional activities of ideation, brainstorming, or prototyping. This is a book for practitioners—for those who have to make things happen, and for those businesses searching for a proven process that leads to real business value. I highly recommend you dig in to this book and use the templates and methodologies to reap the real rewards of innovation."

—John R. Childress, Senior Executive Advisor on leadership, culture and strategy execution issues, Visiting Professor, IE Business School, Madrid

"Innovation can be complicated, messy, and hard to define. This book gives you what you need to make innovation happen and to engage the human beings who do the innovative work"

—John Sweeney, owner of the Brave New Workshop Comedy Theater and author of the bestselling *The Innovative Mindset: 5 Behaviors for Accelerating Breakthroughs*

"In an increasingly rapid changing global economy, firms need to innovate more than ever to survive and thrive. However, many firms fail to innovate since they do not know how to measure or manage it. Patrick Stroh's book, *Advancing Innovation*, offers practical guidelines to help firms organize, strategize, and measure innovation."

—Kevin Linderman, Curtis L. Carlson Professor of Supply Chain & Operations, Carlson School of Management, University of Minnesota

"Advancing Innovation is an exceptional book. Through a holistic perspective, it combines innovation and management techniques in a unique way. This combination is of particular worth, as it gives innovators the freedom to enfold their ideas, while at the same time giving management the tools to control creativity. I liked the combination of helpful practices with the very concrete innovation value scorecard and its clear KPI proposals."

—Janssen, S., Möller, K., Schläfke, M., Director Institute of Accounting, Control and Auditing, Chair of Controlling/Performance Management, University of St. Gallen

"Thank you, Patrick, for writing such a clear and concise roadmap for how corporate finance can add tremendous value in a nontraditional way—through innovation. Yes, finance can and should play in that arena, and this book provides important insights and a simple framework for approaching this goal. It's a quick and compelling read on a subject that grows more important by the day."

—John Kogan, President & CEO, Proformative, Inc.

"Today's CEOs and boards face a real conundrum. Growth expectations are increasing at an accelerating pace. At the same time, shareholders have little appetite for surprises. And missed expectations are often punished by real declines in market value. Finding the right balance of strategy, risk and innovation is key to achieving quality growth. And even the best strategy must be resilient—able to anticipate change and agile enough to adjust quickly. In his book, Patrick Stroh frames the challenge of successfully innovating while managing risk for growth. He provides both insights and examples of how CEOs and their organizations have achieved growth through innovation."

—Dennis Chesley, PwC's Global Risk Consulting Leader and Project Leader for the COSO ERM Framework update

"Patrick Stroh is 100% correct in his assertion that 'Innovation is hard work and perseverance—it's not for the faint of heart.' His blueprint for *Advancing Innovation* is invaluable for those who have the heart and soul for taking risks and raising innovation value."

—Harvey Mackay, author of the #1 New York Times best seller *Swim with the Sharks Without Being Eaten Alive*

"This book in many ways is the first of its kind, dare I say 'innovative,' in that it goes way beyond the abstract to the practical, from the desire to innovate to the capability to innovate for sustainable competitive advantage and growth. The emphasis of this book is unique, focusing on innovation enablement, governance, measurement, and the role of the CFO team. Most organizations face the triple crown threat of competition, consolidation, and commoditization, and *Advancing Innovation* provides real-world implementation advice from someone who has actually done it with success."

—Jeffrey C. Thomson, CMA, CAE, President and CEO, IMA®

"Patrick Stroh's Innovation Value Score® adds an important and powerful new dimension to the domain of innovation, one of the hottest topics in both the private and public sectors for many years. What has been lacking in the dialogue is a rigorous framework for measuring innovation—and without measurement, how do managers know if they are succeeding? Stroh's fresh thinking gives managers the framework and tools they need to evaluate the success of their innovation strategies."

—John McClellan, Managing Director, Thought Leadership, Palladium

"Innovation needs to be at the core of every operational CFO in industry today. With the Innovation Value Score™, Patrick has unleashed a way for financial leaders to measure and govern our effectiveness at innovation. This is a must-read for every CFO looking to take their company to the next level!"

—Benjamin Mulling, CMA, CPA.CITP, CFO, TENTE Casters, Inc.

"Simply competing just won't cut it anymore. This book gives us the guidance to move on to that next level with confidence: innovation. Not easy, but it's essential for success in our faster-than-ever-paced world. Thanks to Patrick and one of our COSO sponsoring organizations, IMA, for getting the dialogue going and giving us some practical examples on how to get started on our innovation journey. This book is just chock-full of ideas and tools to help you drive innovation in your organization. Read it and identify your three gold nuggets as foundational elements for your innovation strategy."

—Robert B. Hirth, Jr., Chairman, Committee of Sponsoring Organizations of the Treadway Commission (COSO)

"在保持企业的可持续发展和引领创新方面，CFO如何更好地发挥洞察力和远见力，并在组织中创造价值形成持续的影响力？ Patrick Stroh先生的Advancing Innovation一书会告诉你答案！"

"In order to maintain sustainable development and lead innovation, how can a CFO better demonstrate the insight and foresight to create value and exert sustained influence in an organization? Mr. Patrick Stroh's book, *Advancing Innovation*, will tell you that answer!"

—Ms. Lixia Tan, 谭丽霞, Senior VP and CFO, Haier Group

Contents

Foreword

David Norton and I introduced the Balanced Scorecard in the early 1990s with several *Harvard Business Review* articles and a 1996 book, *The Balanced Scorecard: Translating Strategy into Action*. Since that time, we wrote four more books as we learned how to extend and apply this powerful framework beyond our original intent—for performance measurement— to help solve an even bigger problem that all organizations had: strategy execution. Faithful adoption of our framework and insights has enabled many organizations to achieve transformational results through successful strategy execution.

In this book, Patrick Stroh has adapted our framework for the measurement and management of innovation. Innovation has been a hot topic for some time now, confirmed in research cited in this book that an overwhelming majority (92%) of respondents feel their organization *should* measure and govern innovation regularly as a key business process for sustaining growth and value. Many of the respondents (71%) work in firms where senior finance and accounting leaders have been asked to support the firm's innovation efforts.

While strategy maps and Balanced Scorecards are typically created and implemented for organizational units, Norton and I have also seen maps and scorecards created for strategic themes that cut across organizational lines.[1] This enables multiple business units and functions to align

---

1 Robert S. Kaplan and David P. Norton, "How to Implement a New Strategy Without Disrupting Your Organization," *Harvard Business Review*, March 2006, pp. 100–109.

around a strategic theme, such as innovation. Successful implementation of an innovation strategy is a team sport, not just the responsibility of the research and development department. It requires active collaboration of multiple units—including R&D, marketing, operations, finance, and customer service—that often find it difficult to work from the same page. That is why creating and agreeing to objectives and metrics is so powerful for aligning the organization around the execution of an innovation strategy.

I discussed with the author and his constituents about how the balanced scorecard framework can and should be applied to business innovation. Especially important is to strive to create tight causal linkages between the strategic objectives on a strategy map and associated metrics on the Balanced Scorecard. I explained why we prefer not to weight the metrics in our scorecards, except when absolutely essential, such as when linking performance to compensation. I'm pleased to see much of this counsel implemented in this book and in the associated Innovation Value Score® (IVS) measurement platform. The goal is not to use the scorecard to calculate a single measure of success for a complex strategy, but to have managers use multiple indicators to guide their company's success in executing its business strategy, much as how a skilled pilot uses the multiple indicators in the cockpit to guide the plane for a successful journey.

I certainly support using the Balanced Scorecard framework to measure, and more importantly *manage*, how innovation is accomplished in your company. I hope you find the framework articulated in this book helpful, and good luck in your innovation journey.

Robert S. Kaplan

Book Registration

Congratulations! By purchasing this book, you have also purchased a license to use many of the forms and templates that are discussed and outlined in this book. This book is meant to be a source that you can use to quickly come up to speed on innovation best practices, execution, and measurement. Sometimes, one of the hardest parts in taking the next step forward after reading a book like this is how to implement the concepts and, simply, where to begin when you are at work. To help with that, I have created templates and forms from the discussions throughout this book, which are available at www.innovationvaluescore.com for you to download, place your own company logo on, modify as you see fit, and begin to use immediately. I hope these are helpful to you and will help jumpstart your efforts.

To register your book, e-mail IMA® (Institute of Management Accountants) at research@imanet.org for a registration code. Then visit www.innovationvaluescore.com and enter the registration code into the "Advancing Innovation Templates" tab. The forms will be activated for your use.

Also on this website you will find other resources that may be helpful in your innovation efforts, including information on an Innovation Value Score® (IVS) system subscription for "*Helping Organizations* **Accelerate Innovation** *with* **Actionable Reporting & Comparable Measures** *for Results*!" which is described in detail later in this book.

Enjoy, and good luck in your innovation execution!

Introduction

The greatest danger for most of us is not that our aim is too high and we miss it, but that it is too low and we reach it.

— Michelangelo

Everyone talks about "it"—Innovation. We all talk about its significance, how we have it, and how we are striving for more of it. It has become a rather maligned term that means many different things to people. One similarity, though, is that everyone wants innovation in their company and wants to be seen in their market space and by their customers as innovative leaders. Yet the nature of innovation, its substance, is very vague—or at least, very different depending on the context, industry, or landscape.

Even when we can agree on what innovation is, we have no standard way to measure its results. How can you say you are innovative or a leader in innovation if you can't measure innovation? If you can't measure innovation in a comparable way against others, it's hard to know who is innovative and who is just talking platitudes. Being "innovative" is akin to the term "strategic." We all want people to see us and our businesses as strategic, we know we need to be strategic to be successful, and constituents ask us about how our strategic efforts are playing out. And similar to innovation, there are a ton of different yardsticks on how to measure—and even define—being strategic.

By picking up this book and beginning to read, I hope you agree that the topic of innovation is worthy of your time and critical thinking. Let's start with a basic hypothesis of what innovation is and have a meaningful discussion around innovation that is relevant, consistent, value-based, meaningful, important, *and* that creates real value for customers and stakeholders! In its simplest form, I believe innovation is about this last factor—creating real value for customers and stakeholders.

INNOVATION THAT CREATES REAL VALUE FOR CUSTOMERS AND STAKEHOLDERS

Often, when people think of innovation, they think of technology, patents, and new products. All are innovative, but they are just a *part* of innovation. If you only look at new technologies introduced, the number of patents filed, or the number of new products introduced to market, you haven't measured any realized "value." Yes, all of those things are important—and I'd suggest they are a part of innovation and part of the measuring of innovation value—but if all those new technologies, patents, and new products generate zero dollars of revenue or value, do we really care?

Therefore, I suggest that innovation can be defined and measured by the value we create along the way for our customers and stakeholders. Additionally, there is not one singular initiative or program you can put in place to be "innovative." It is an amalgamation of initiatives and measures around value creation, and they can vary from organization to organization.

Innovation is required in our organizations at a faster pace than ever. But being innovative and driving innovation value in your organization is not an overnight transformation, nor does it have to take years to develop. Innovation must be implemented, monitored, and measured very thoughtfully and from a viewpoint of driving customer value. Anytime you are innovating, simply ask, "Is this going to drive value to our customers, and would they pay for it?" This serves as a good acid test—it doesn't cover everything that needs to be asked or considered, but it's a good gut check. You could be innovating business processes that the customer may have no knowledge about, but if it ultimately improves the end product—the quality, the speed of delivery, the cost, the longevity, or another important factor—then the customer should see value in it. That is worth innovating around. As you consider innovation initiatives, decisions, and measures, always keep the customer and your go-to-market value proposition front of mind.

NEW RESEARCH CONDUCTED BY IMA®

The field of management accounting and the job of the CFO (chief financial officer) continues to evolve. CFOs are being asked to take on more and more responsibilities in their execution and oversight roles. It wasn't that long ago that CFOs were getting tapped by the CEO (chief executive officer) to do more of the strategy planning in organizations. Now, similarly, CFOs and their staffs are being asked to get involved with innovation. But to what degree is that involvement, and do you think this is an anomaly only in one industry, geography, or size of company? IMA and I had the same question, so we conducted market research to get specific facts and findings on how the role of finance is evolving in regards to innovation management and leadership. In June and July 2015, IMA sent a survey to its professional members who are CFOs, corporate officers, controllers, directors, and accounting managers in the United States, Canada, Europe, Middle East, Africa, and Asia/Pacific. The results confirmed many of our assumptions and produced even stronger, more pronounced feedback than anticipated. The following tables provide some demographic characteristics of the respondents—you will find a very encompassing diversity in the participants that leads to global, all-inclusive findings.

Industry. Which of the following best describes your organization?

	No.	%
Manufacturing: Aerospace, Automotive, all other Manufacturing	80	29.5%
Business Services: Advertising, Banking, Consulting, Financial Services, Legal, Publishing	46	17.0%
Institutions: Government, Education, Not-for-Profit	32	11.8%
Retail: Apparel, Consumer Packaged Goods (CPG), Wholesale/Retail	26	9.6%
Technology: Biotech, Computer, Software, Technology, Telecom	18	6.6%
Healthcare: Facilities, Payers, Providers, Supporting Products and Services	12	4.4%
Other	55	20.3%
Not answered	2	0.7%
Total	**271**	**100.0%**

Location. Where is your business unit primarily located?

	No.	%
United States	138	50.9%
Middle East	65	24.0%
Asia/Pacific	45	16.6%
Europe	13	4.8%
Africa	6	2.2%
Canada	3	1.1%
Not answered	1	0.4%
Total	**271**	**100.0%**

Revenues. What is your organization's annual revenues (or budget, if it's a nonprofit or governmental entity) in U.S. dollars?

	No.	%
$0–$5 million	47	17.5%
$5 million–$100 million	104	38.8%
$100 million–$1 billion	52	19.4%
$1 billion–$5 billion	28	10.4%
$5 billion+	37	13.8%
Total	**268**	**100.0%**

This symbol appears throughout the book to introduce facts, opinions, analysis, or direct responses from the IMA research on innovation that was conducted during June and July 2015.

10 Key Findings

Below is a list of the 10 key findings from the IMA research. The full survey can be found in the Appendix, including the respondents' demographics and the results for each question. Salient points will also be referenced throughout the book as they are relevant to the specific discussion.

1. 92% of respondents said their organization should measure and govern innovation regularly as a key business process to sustain growth and value → *Yes, innovation is important!*

2. 75% said they needed to significantly evolve or reinvent their business value proposition every five years at minimum to maintain relevance and market value. → *The longevity of your value proposition is shrinking, and it must be updated faster than in the past.*

3. 37% said they needed to evolve/reinvent their value proposition not just every five years, but every one to three years. → *Some industries are changing faster than others, but let's be clear, we are ALL changing faster now than at any other point in history.*

4. 57% said they don't formally measure innovation success/value → *92% see the value in measuring innovation, but almost 60% don't do it—likely because innovation is hard to measure or they don't know how.*

5. 67% of senior finance and accounting professionals now support innovation in some fashion vs. only 35% 10 years ago → *Finance leaders are being asked, but do they have the skill set to support and lead innovation?*

6. Respondents predicted that number to go up six more percentage points to 73% in just another three years! → *If you're a CFO or senior finance and accounting leader and haven't yet been asked to support or lead innovation, you soon will be!*

7. Only 52% of companies get innovation ideas from their employees, and 31% get innovations from their suppliers—while 43% and 40% would *like to* get ideas from these sources, respectively, but are not doing so. → *Where are organizations getting innovation ideas from, or are they simply not asking anyone?*

8. When asked if innovation discussion should occur in the normal business processes of budgeting, capital planning, operational reviews and/or strategic planning—responses were 69%, 64%,

69%, and 88%, respectively, that innovation discussion should be occurring in those forums throughout the business as it currently operates. → *Innovation needs to be embedded in the organization, not implemented and conducted separately.*

9. When asked where they would need the most innovation improvement support to lead and support innovation, 60% of respondents said they would need help in all three named areas (Galvanizing, Enabling, and Measurement). → *There is much work to do, but this book will help show you how.*

10. Respondents' industry, location, or company size had little statistical impact on the survey responses and trends. → *The trends transcended all demographics.*

The diversity in the participants' industry, size, and geography make for truly global, all-inclusive findings. As you read about the collective thoughts of the participants throughout the book, note many of the similarities in their responses and insights. Innovation is an important issue everywhere.

HOW THIS BOOK IS ORGANIZED

This book is divided into four parts. Part I introduces the idea that every business needs to innovate, and the three chapters that make up this section focus on the concept of "innovation governance" and why that term is not an oxymoron but extremely relevant and important. They address the concept of "important innovation"—because not all innovation is necessarily important and can be distracting and dilutive to the business rather than helpful and accretive. Lastly they'll identify some of the roles and responsibilities for those who need to support and/or lead innovation initiatives in their organizations. Chapter 3, in particular, may be an eye opener for the senior finance and accounting professionals—as you see just how well-suited you are to support and lead innovation efforts. This section is geared toward the office of the CFO and senior finance and accounting professionals, but if that is not you, there is still relevance in reading through these traits and the strengths required to be successful in innovation.

Parts II, III, and IV describe the three elements of the Innovation Elixir® that will lead you to innovation success! Sometimes when people have a special process or "mixture" of how to achieve success, they call it their "secret sauce." Other times you hear about people or businesses looking to find the missing piece to solve the puzzle of success. I refer to my secret sauce or missing piece that leads to innovation success as the "Innovation Elixir." Why? Because there are a few basic principles when you concoct an elixir. First, an elixir has a few base elements that must be included, or it won't work. Second, the elements must be mixed in the appropriate proportions, but those change from time to time and from circumstance to circumstance. And third, no two elixirs are exactly the same — kind of like that favorite culinary dish that your family has passed down through three generations! There is a basic recipe to create the dish, but everyone has their own specific version and interpretation of how to best prepare it. Creating an Innovation Elixir in your company to drive innovation value is exactly like this. It has some base elements that are required, but then you need to change the proportions of the elements and add a few specific ingredients of your own to achieve the ultimate elixir that will work in your business, your industry, and your current business landscape.

Parts II, III, and IV of the book unpack the three elements of the base Innovation Elixir. You'll find that the elements are sequential to begin with, then require continuous review, monitoring, and tweaking as you begin and then maintain your innovation journeys. This bears repeating — when you are first introducing innovation efforts, the three elements of the Innovation Elixir are sequential. You need to do them in proper order to be successful. There are no shortcuts. Once you have gone through all three elements, they become part of a continuous cycle in which you monitor, maintain, and augment each of the elements to ensure innovation success. These three elements of the base Innovation Elixir are:

Galvanizing, Enabling, and Measuring

Think of it like exploring and mining *gems* in your business — not just *thinking* about innovation, but setting up for, executing, and measuring innovation value and then taking actions based on those measures to create even more value!

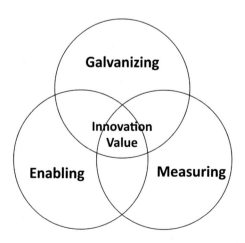

You could also think about the three elements of Innovation Elixir like a Venn diagram. At the convergence of those three elements, you obtain the value. Can you get any value in doing only one of the elements? Sure. But it won't be systematic, repeatable, and lasting in your organization. It will be more a function of luck than enablement and leadership.

What did research respondents say was their biggest area of concern and focus for improvement with regard to innovation? Thirty-seven percent were almost equally split between *galvanizing*, *enabling*, and *measuring*, with a slight edge to those who wanted help in *enabling*. But 60% responded "all of the above," wanting help in all three areas if they were going to be responsible and accountable for innovation value and governance in their organization. That's smart. As the three areas were defined to them, they saw the importance of each one as well as the need to solidify their own knowledge in each area.

Part III specifically gets into the "how to" of innovation success: Chapters 6–10 describe five channels of innovation you can implement in your organizations and give you the specifics on the innovation channels. I'll cover how to implement these channels quickly while also pointing out pitfalls to watch out for, how to measure success in the channel, and how to make it an innovation channel that endures over time. Some organizations may be more skewed to certain channels than others, but you should consider the multiple channels presented in Chapters 6–10. Determine which apply to your business and where you can drive innovation value — incremental, distinctive, and breakthrough innovations!

Part IV of the book describes the third element of the Innovation Elixir: measurement of innovation. If we can measure it, we can improve it! Measurement is important so that we can get better at innovation, get more innovation, and, therefore, drive more value. Chapters 11–13 discuss strategic business archetypes and what your firm looks most like from a business strategy standpoint.

Part IV also introduces you to Innovation Value Score® (IVS). I have a simple goal and purpose for IVS. I want everyone in the world to be more successful in their innovation endeavors and benefit from using IVS to *measure* their innovation results and *manage* their value creation. While there is no perfect singular metric to measure innovation success in all organizations, I believe IVS can serve as a start to look at the right balance of indicators, correlate those indicators to your business strategy, allow you to compare and contrast to other organizations, and, most important, take meaningful action to drive value. Keep in mind: *IVS is not about just measurement; it is about overall innovation value creation and management!*

Although IVS may not be perfect, it will be directionally correct—you aren't calculating earnings per share to three decimal places, you're looking for directional leading indicators and mile markers. It enables a meaningful dialogue and discussion around innovation within your businesses, your industries, and in local and global economies. By creating this measurement system, I wanted to enable you, my readers, to drive more value for your customers and stakeholders. You can and should look at the world like a growing pie chart in which you can continue to grow with additional value, rather than a static pie chart where everyone fights over market share. I aspire to help all businesses and organizations to drive more innovation value and realize more value! Yes, it's a lofty goal, but it's a worthy goal.

As you read through this book, bear in mind that I did not write this book with the intent of holding it up as new revolutionary thinking in the theory of innovation. There are plenty of luminaries out there who can speak and write extensively about innovation theory. Rather, I wrote this book to provide a "how-to" approach that enhances your practices in innovation and increases the probability of success by laying out baseline innovation information with a multitude of foundational elements from many places.

Then we can focus on the new thinking in this body of work, which is *how to effectively measure* innovation. If we can't measure it, we can't improve it. And we want a measurement system that we can compare and contrast against other organizations so that we can drive everyone's innovation levels up, therefore increasing value in our markets.

Finally, the Appendix offers some very valuable tools that are referenced throughout the text. How often do you go to a seminar, webinar, or read a book, and you'd like to ask that author or presenter, "Can you show me an example of a form I could use to capture/evaluate/communicate the concept you just covered?" You get the concept, but can't they just show you a template or form you could use to implement the idea? Well, in this book, the answer is YES! As you read through the chapters, you'll see references to best practices, pros and cons, process steps, check lists, decision flows, and the like. The Appendix has an inventory of several of these documents for you to review.

On top of that, purchasing this book also gives you online access to some these forms NOW! The forms are available for download at www.innovationvaluescore.com. (See the book registration page at the front of the book.) You can download the forms and use them in your business now! You are welcome (and in many cases encouraged) to modify them according to your business environment, culture, and specific needs.

Download these templates to start working on the some of the processes, innovation channels, and checklists right away.

And be sure to check back from time to time for updated or new templates as you continue to build and enhance your own tools. I hope these templates are helpful to jumpstart your innovation execution!

GETTING TO YES

There are a number of conclusions you are likely to take away from reading this book. These are the keys to galvanizing, enabling, and measuring—keep them in mind as you are reading.

Galvanizing Keys

- When setting the tone and galvanizing the organization to be ready for innovation efforts, remember that relationships matter and are a key to success. Consider the shadow you cast. Be a leader that sets the right tone at the top—a tone that stresses the importance of balance both in risk and rewards.

- Employees frequently perceive finance and accounting executives as focusing only on "cost reduction." Make sure that it is clear what happens with cost savings. Also ensure that not all business challenges or other innovation initiatives are centered on cost reduction. Cost reduction is good, but costs and efficiencies are only one focus area.

- Don't take on a cultural challenge all by yourself! If you need to implement some change or provide clarity on cultural norms and expectations, you may need to do this work first in order that subsequent innovation value can be achieved. Implementing world class tools and mechanisms in an environment that isn't ready, supportive, or tolerant of them will only lead to failure. Be sure you have galvanized appropriately!

- While we always want the CEO to show support for any new effort or project, I believe it is a must-have with regard to innovation—especially if your company has a hard driving, performance-oriented culture. Failure typically is not accepted, and people know that. The CEO needs to stand up and say, "We still value being a high-performance company, and in doing so, we need to be better at taking calculated risks. We want to support innovation efforts, and we realize that will sometimes lead to failure. It's okay to fail—just fail fast and learn from it. We will be better off in the long run and create more value." Steve Jobs said, "*Sometimes when you innovate, you make mistakes. It is best to admit them quickly and get on with improving your other innovations."* Imagine your CEO making a statement similar to this to the troops. It's permission to try and fail, yet a reminder to be thoughtful and careful. Whatever the specific message, the tone comes from the top. Set the tone!

Enabling Keys

- When you begin to enable the company to innovate, be aware of the differences: different people, different companies, different leaders, and different channels. Recognize and respect these various differences, account for them in your design and implementation of innovation channels, and capitalize on your business's strengths.

- Be aware of your employees' biggest strengths and how best to leverage them. Implementing multiple innovation channels is a good way to do this. Different employees and functional areas have different natural skills and strengths, and they will respond to these channels differently.

- Many people can be creative given the right environment and some encouragement. For example, front-line folks, those closest to the customer, have ideas based on what they see every day. Tap into these people and find ways to make them feel good about sharing and innovating!

- Communicate, communicate, and communicate to *enable* the organization. Don't let ideas or submissions of any kind go into a "black hole."

- When you try multiple channels, not all may succeed. Try, test, adjust, succeed, or fail, and then move forward. Don't be impatient; give them a chance, but don't beat a dead horse.

Measuring Keys

- When measuring innovation, the old adage applies, "Garbage in equals garbage out." When implementing innovation channels and programs, consider data integrity, the ability of having repeatable capture processes and reporting of that information, and clarity in measuring and calculating innovation value.

- If you don't measure, you can't improve. And if you don't share the results after you measure, nobody knows or understands the results, leading to (usually negative) speculation. Measure, improve, share, and repeat!

- Sharing with "the street" (public constituents) is another matter. Be smart, honest, and thoughtful in distinguishing between internal and confidential intelligence vs. information that is ready to be shared more broadly, just like in any other reporting you prepare.

- Measuring innovation has historically not been easy. IVS is meant to help give finance, accounting, and all leaders a standard innovation system to use as a yardstick to better measure, compare, and improve innovation levels and give them clear actions to take. Try it and see if it better defines innovation value and pinpoints areas in which you can drive more business value for your constituents.

- Beginning to measure results is the beginning, not the end. Measuring doesn't just tell you who won the game; it tells you if you are winning or losing in the larger game of fulfilling your vision and achieving your mission.

We all can work on our tendency to say no and find more ways to "get to yes," especially if it drives value in our organizations. There is a great insight in *Innovation at the Speed of Laughter*: *"When we say yes first, we are not saying we should approve a budget, staffing or the idea will be automatically implemented."* Give yourself permission to say "Yes" to an idea and explore it a bit. The rigorous evaluation can come later.

As you begin to read through this book, find ways to GET TO YES in your thinking, application, and adoption of these processes and recommendations. Getting to yes translates to getting to innovation value creation in your organization—and isn't value creation at the core of why your organization exists?

PART I

Innovation—A Call to Action

Some men look at things the way they are and ask why? I
dream of things that are not and ask why not?
                                                    —Robert Kennedy

I believe the call to action around innovation has never been stronger than it is today. Why? Because in addition to IMA's research on innovation, there is other research and discussion that talks about how companies wish they could innovate more, better, and faster and generate more value creation. A 2015 McKinsey poll stated that *"94% of the managers surveyed said they were dissatisfied with their company's innovation performance."*[1] And 3M has declared that *"Innovation is a survival issue."*[2] Clearly, as businesses look inside their four walls, they are not happy and feel the pressure to innovate.

But the really scary fact of this call to action is what is happening externally. The world is moving faster than ever before! It seems like every generation says "We are going through a rate of change faster than ever before." I think that has probably been true—technology, globalization, and other factors have had us on a perpetual treadmill that seems to go faster and faster each year, month, week, and day! A general rule of thumb in business used to be that you need to reinvent your value proposition about every 10 years to stay relevant, profitable, and competitive. Of course that varies from industry to industry, and disruptive technologies, legislation, and political environments can all cause turbulence; but, as a rule, 10 years was about average. New research says the 10-year rule is dead, that the new rule is you need to reinvent your business and value proposition about every five years, which correlates with the IMA research.[3]

Five years!!! The research doesn't say you have to totally reinvent yourself and introduce new breakthrough innovations and products every five years, but if you are not advancing your core value proposition after five years, you are going to be a shrinking business and less relevant. Your best days will be behind you, not in front of you. McKinsey also lightly touched on this fact when it said, *"In the digital age, the pace of change has gone into hyper speed, so companies must get these strategic, creative, executional and organizational factors right to innovate successfully."*[4] Many thought leaders are saying it: The world is moving faster than ever before. The question is: How are you reacting and adapting to this change?

You may ask yourself, "As a finance leader, why is this a call to action for me?" Because finance is not an independent discipline; it needs to be managed and led in tandem with all other disciplines in an organization. In the worst case, finance and accounting can dominate strategy and stifle innovation. In the best case, finance and accounting can be a leader of innovation and a driver of successful achievement of strategy and mission. If finance leadership is not involved either in a direct leadership role or in a very strong support capacity, innovation efforts are going to have a far lesser chance of being successful—and almost zero chance of having any long-term staying power and influence in an organization. Finance, strategy, and innovation are inextricably linked, and finance and accounting leaders need to have a role in innovation governance in order to help and lead our businesses in value creation.

 This call to action and the importance of innovation is validated by the feedback IMA received:

- 67% of respondents agreed or strongly agreed that innovation *is* a key focus in their organization's strategy.

- 92% agreed or strongly agreed that innovation *should be* a key focus in their strategy.

- But 47% agreed or strongly agreed that while their organization wants to innovate, short-term financial risks and goals get in the way. Another 25% were neutral. That means only 28% truly make innovation a priority and don't push it to the side to get short-term results.

Businesses need stronger leadership around innovation and a way to measure results and value. Otherwise, they'll continue to push their innovation initiatives to the side when pressured for short-term results. You know it's important and is key to your strategy, so let's focus on how to execute and how to measure to drive results.

Consider the opening quote by Robert Kennedy again: "*Some men look at things the way they are and ask why? I dream of things that are not and ask why not?*" Yes, dream. Dream big, dream small, dream in all shapes and sizes! Consider things as they are and challenge the status quo. But don't just be a dreamer. Be a disciplined, multifaceted dreamer, facilitator, and leader who empowers others to dream and, therefore, innovate. Innovation is a team sport! Innovation can't be about one person sitting in a think tank dreaming up ideas.

While I love the Kennedy quote as a great example and reminder to stretch our thinking from the current state, I also believe the quote can be a disservice by suggesting that people see innovation as only something dreamers can do. We ALL can innovate! We ALL can create value!

With a desire to innovate and many data points telling us we better innovate or get left behind, let's discuss in Part I what is really needed for innovation to succeed. Let's consider what kind of innovation we want to promote and get from our employees and other stakeholders and then define the skill set we'll need to make it all happen!

CHAPTER 1

Innovation Governance

Innovation is creativity with a job to do.

—John Emmerling

Innovation governance. It sounds like an oxymoron, doesn't it? Trust me, the first time I said those two words, they just didn't feel or sound right. Then after some "fierce conversation" with a good friend and colleague of mine, I started to see this combination in a different light. In further spirited discussions with others on the topic, I then saw the need to explain and make the case for better innovation governance in our businesses.

My own background has had both governance in my early finance and accounting years and innovation in my later years running businesses and serving on executive teams. Whenever I look back at the times I researched and executed successful innovation, I realize that more and more of that innovation success came to be because of good governance!

Random epiphanies and great ideas don't need governance, but they are just that—random. But systematic, holistic, continuous innovation at a larger scale and from a multitude of sources in your business and value chain does require and thrive with governance!

Consider the opening quote again: "*Innovation is creativity with a job to do.*" If you think about it, this really describes innovation governance. You need to be creative and ideate new solutions, but you need to execute with discipline to achieve the value. Simply said, you need both sides of the equation!

Innovation = Creativity and Ideation

Governance = Execution and Discipline

Do you see the need to measure and govern innovation? When IMA asked respondents that question, it ended up being the strongest response in the entire survey: 92% said their organization should measure and govern innovation regularly as a key business process to sustain growth and value. 92%! The downside to this was that only 44% of respondents agreed or strongly agreed that they set innovation goals in their business, and even a lower percentage, only 35%, used innovation measures specifically to measure performance. So we know we need to innovate—it's clearly important, but it is hard to measure. Ultimately, how do you "govern" innovation, and who should be doing that? Keep reading...

WHO IS RESPONSIBLE FOR INNOVATION?

Not that long ago, the title "Chief Innovation Officer" would have been sneered at as a made-up or lofty title with very little real responsibility in an organization. That's no longer the case, as one Director of Innovation Strategy, Harvey Wade, explains: "Due to greater competition, tightened budgets, and new technology, the importance assigned to innovation as a legitimate and vital business process has been elevated in recent years. This has placed a newfound importance of whoever's responsibility it is to ensure innovation is being encouraged and helping to deliver results... Globalization, the recession, and the fact consumers have more information available to them has certainly created a more crowded and competitive business landscape. Companies are under huge pressure to evolve at a new pace, stay ahead on a realistic budget [i.e., do more with less], and squeeze as much as possible out of what they've got."[5]

In short, companies need to execute their current offerings as best as possible to aid in funding new improvements and ventures. This requires constant innovation.

Wade goes on to say:

> "To ensure consistent and meaningful progress, decision makers within companies must ask the right questions about the current state of the organization, the industry, and where they are both heading—seemingly obvious analysis [that] many businesses fail to do adequately.

> "Finding answers to these questions, and solutions to the issues they raise, is even less frequently mastered. This process extends beyond the decision makers or boardroom, and its success relies on the effective use of an already existing asset of the organization—its people.

> "Within business departments, incremental innovation is common, but especially in large or diverse organizations, someone is needed to manage the transformational strategic innovation that straddles the entire business, [and that person needs to have] buy-in from the CEO [who is traditionally responsible for business direction and strategy] and [who] can galvanize the whole workforce [to consistently and systematically provide innovation value.]"[6]

Who is responsible for innovation in your company? Do you have a Chief Innovation Officer? A Director of Innovation? Do you have an "Innovation Council" or group of innovation champions throughout your business?

> **In Chinese philosophy, the yin and yang describe how apparently opposite or contrary forces are actually complementary.**

The answers to these questions vary from company to company and most of the time are dictated by size. In many *Fortune* 100 companies, you'll find a Chief Innovation Officer. Sometimes you'll find this title combined with business strategy like one of my prior positions, Chief Strategy & Innovation Officer. Other times, it is shared responsibly across an Innovation Council or some sort of steering committee rather than a single person. How you centralize or decentralize the roles and responsibilities for innovation leadership can vary, but you have to cover them one way or another. This chapter focuses on what the responsibilities are.

WHAT IS INNOVATION GOVERNANCE?

What is innovation governance? Wouldn't governance stifle innovation and creativity? Isn't the problem with big companies that they have too much governance and not enough innovation? On the flip side, maybe you have worked really hard to put appropriate and prudent governance in place, and now someone is telling you to combine innovation with that? That just doesn't seem to make sense—but keep reading because it makes perfect sense.

In Chinese philosophy, the yin and yang describe how apparently opposite or contrary forces are actually complementary.

This philosophy embodies *innovation governance* in a single sentence. Innovation and governance feel like, sound like, and show up in business like opposite forces. Governance is about control and measurement. Governance even sounds structured, hierarchical, and slow. But proper governance in just about any business will produce better, sustainable results and value creation. McKinsey noted, "*Since innovation is a complex, company-wide endeavor, it requires a set of crosscutting practices and processes to structure, organize, and encourage it.*"[7] This last part of the statement "...to structure, organize, and encourage..." speaks to *innovation governance*. Innovation is about creativity and ideas. Innovation is about fighting the status quo and doing things in a better, cheaper, faster way or even doing different things altogether. But innovation is also about discipline and process.

So how is the combination of these two opposing forces helpful? First, let's consider the term and concept of governance.

Governance has been defined as follows:

> *The lawful control over the affairs of a unit.[8] It is the establishment of policies and continuous monitoring of their proper implementation, by the members of the governing body of an organization. It includes the mechanisms required to balance the powers of the members (with the associated accountability), and their primary duty of enhancing the prosperity and viability of the organization.*
>
> *Synonyms include: administration, care, charge, control, direction, government, guidance, handling, intendance, management, operation, oversight, presidency, regulation, running, stewardship, superintendence, superintendency, supervision.[9]*

That sounds like a lot of structure! Process, structure, execution, testing, measuring, and repeat. To some of us, structure is good because it's predictable, provides boundaries and guidelines, and leads to results. But like a pendulum that swings back and forth, if you swing too far in a governance direction, all those good things can create imbalance and poor results. This is where innovation comes in.

Innovation is defined as:

> *The process of translating an idea or invention into a good or service that creates value or for which customers will pay. To be called an innovation, an idea must be replicable at an economical cost and must satisfy a specific need. Innovation involves deliberate application of information, imagination and initiative in deriving greater or different values from resources, and includes all processes by which new ideas are generated and converted into useful products.*
>
> *In business, innovation often results when ideas are applied by the company in order to further satisfy the needs and expectations of the customers. In a social context, innovation helps create new methods for alliance creation, joint venturing, flexible work hours, and creation of buyers' purchasing power.*
>
> *Innovations are sometimes divided into two broad categories of evolutionary innovations, which are brought about by many incremental advances in technology or processes, and revolutionary innovations (also called discontinuous innovations), which are often disruptive and new.[10]*

From this definition, you can easily see how innovation is an opposing force to governance. Governance is meant to reduce risk in a business, whereas innovation can be seen as synonymous with risk-taking in order to evolve and, in some cases, create a revolution to develop new products, markets, and business value. Innovation is flexing, evolving, failing, and trying again.

When you consider innovation and governance *together*, now you can start to think in these terms. Innovation governance is vital to organizations that are true innovators or aspiring innovators. Innovation is either a one-hit wonder in some cases or public relations to impress your board, customers, shareholders, and/or the media in other cases. However, innovation *governance* means, for example, that the oversight body ensures there is internal capacity to deliver on innovation, including funding, roles, incentives, and more. It is about making innovation *sustainable* as opposed to a one-off that then is exposed to the chopping block when times get tough. This governance should ensure there is a balance of varied innovation efforts in play that are managed holistically as a portfolio. The overall result of this innovation portfolio is about its value creation — allowing for wins and losses of individual projects. Applying the appropriate level of structure within your organization should actually empower and accelerate innovation, not stifle it.

Innovation governance is like setting rules in a soccer game. Tell the participants the rules, and let them execute. Don't make it burdensome and complicated. Make the boundaries clear and then stand back! When you put these two opposing forces together, you create a value that is greater than the sum of its parts.

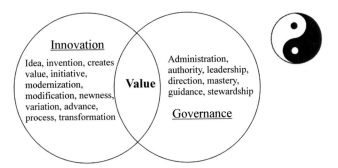

Applying structure and discipline to creativity is obviously not a new concept. The bigger issue is not *if* you should do this, but *how* you combine these two philosophies to drive value. Additionally, we need to be cognizant as to how the marriage of these two philosophies and approaches will culminate and drive value in our businesses. This is not a one-size-fits-all answer, but an amalgamation that we must arrive at.

HOW DO WE GOVERN INNOVATION?

There are three elements of innovation success:

1. *Galvanizing* the organization for innovation success;

2. *Enabling* the organization to solicit, capture, evaluate, and implement innovation projects and ideas; and

3. *Measuring* innovation value and success.

These elements are discussed in much greater detail in Part II of this book; however, the next sections of this chapter introduce these concepts to show how they fit into the topic of innovation governance.

> **Skills of an innovation leader include being facilitative and consultative.**

Galvanizing

Innovation leaders are responsible for establishing an innovation language so everyone on the team is working toward the same goals. By fulfilling this duty, the innovation leader helps the company develop a clear understanding of what innovation means within the context of the company and its industry. The guesswork is removed, so when one person speaks on innovation, everyone else should understand the language and have a shared idea of what the innovation will require.

Even *galvanizing* the organization for innovation success is only the beginning. You need to constantly monitor and adapt processes and tools to drive innovation value. As with many other strategic initiatives, innovation governance requires solid change management.

Galvanizing the organization can be summarized as effectively structuring, organizing, and encouraging the organization for success. When done effectively, it should serve to accelerate your business strategies.

Enabling

Many business people agree with the old adage that "good ideas can come from anywhere." The innovation leader often has the duty of providing structure for budding thoughts and innovations. This means managing the submissions of inventive ideas and setting up a protocol for testing and reviewing them. Whether the team is a small group or an entire department, having a structure can encourage more creativity since everyone involved will be seeking results. As discussed in

Part III, *enabling* your organization is not a "one-channel-works-for-all endeavor." Companies are different. They have different cultures, employees, risk tolerances, and different ways of getting things done. A successful innovation channel in one company may be very different from a successful innovation channel in another company. But basic innovation channels can be tweaked to be successful in just about any business.

Measuring

At the end of the day, businesses can't and shouldn't just innovate because it sounds good or because it's in vogue to have an "innovation center" to show off to visitors. Companies need to produce measureable value creation! Now, not every project and every idea has to produce a positive result—if they do, you aren't taking enough risk and should likely be stretching for more. You have to be willing to fail and get back in the saddle and try again. But in the end, you need to have generated results and value across your entire body of work as a whole or your innovation is likely for naught.

In all three of these areas—galvanizing, enabling, and measuring—you need to apply two related, but different, skill sets: *management* and *leadership*. Here's how they differ:

- *Management is a set of processes that can keep a complicated system of people and technology running smoothly.*

- *Leadership is a set of processes that creates organizations in the first place or adapts them to significantly changing circumstances.*

- *Successful transformation is 70%–90% leadership and only 10%–30% management.*[11]

This gives us an interesting starting point on innovation governance. Innovation governance certainly needs to include both management and leadership, but in what proportion, and where should we focus? Of course, the answer is "it depends on the business." But we can suggest that the appropriate mix is probably the inverse of what is needed in transformation: It's probably closer to 70% management and 30% leadership. Why? Because you want to ingrain innovation channels, ideation, execution, monitoring, and other activities as deep into the organization as possible, and that takes day-to-day management and execution. Although leadership at the top is critical and should not be taken for granted—because without it, the management and execution may be fruitless—the bias in this equation should be on *execution*.

CHARACTERISTICS AND ROLES OF THE INNOVATION LEADER

So what exactly should an innovation leader embody? What would I look for in the person I want to lead and drive innovation at my company? The following is a representation of the characteristics and traits that innovation leaders should have and aspire to have:

Strategic Agility—be strategically aware and able to execute tactically in the short term, but also have an eye on long-term strategic planning. I like to call this "Short-term Focus, Long-term View." *Facilitation Skills*— believe in the benefits of innovation, but not necessarily be the creative, innovative thinker. In most cases, the innovation leader actually *should not be* the creative thinker or, at least, should not be the *only* creative thinker.

Organizational Agility—create an environment that values, allows, and enables innovators to operate and succeed. To facilitate this, be organizationally savvy and understand influence and power relationships within and across functional areas.

Organizational Influence—be a "powerful" executive who can counterbalance the natural biases of business units and functional areas when it comes to change and new innovation ideas.

Consultative —be consultative to innovators and leaders by asking questions that continue to peel back the onion to the layers of value, by setting up innovators for success by recalling historical efforts (wins and losses), and by providing insights on functional relationships and interdependencies, turbulence, or other factors the innovators may not be considering.

Inside/Outside Views—have a watchful eye on internal developments, initiatives, and improvements while keeping an external eye on customer loyalty, retention, satisfaction, and needs. Always be considering new projects, new markets, new partnerships, and alliances to look at value creation and expediency.

Excellent Communication Skills—be able to communicate in many forms and with many constituents both inside and outside the company. That does not mean you need to be a "Master of Creativity or Ideas." The role of innovation leader includes the above elements as well as being able to communicate effectively. How many people do you know are good at relating to the challenges of front-line employees and can also talk to a Wall Street analyst, a CEO, a key supplier, and so on? It's a master communicator!

In a McKinsey study, innovation leaders were asked what they do well.[12] Across the eight factors, "aspire," "discover," and "mobilize" came to the top. Areas that ranked lowest included "choose" and "evolve." Each of us makes choices and evolves every day in our companies' various processes (see the interdependencies discussion in Chapter 11). So why do we struggle in these areas in regards to innovation—to choose and evolve? If you apply innovation governance in your company in the way I discuss it in this book, you could improve in these areas.

Others in the field have made similar lists of what an innovation leader should do, such as:

- Be adept at using innovation tools.

- Create frequent opportunities for blue-sky thinking.

- Avoid premature judgments when evaluating new options.

- Demonstrate an appetite for unconventional ideas.

- Recognize innovators and celebrate "smart failures."

- Personally mentor innovation teams.

- Free up time and money for innovation.

- Hire and promote for creativity.

- Work to eliminate bureaucratic impediments to innovation.

- Understand and apply the principles of rapid prototyping and low-cost experimentation.[13]

The important point is that nowhere on this list or any other list of suggested traits for an innovation leader does it say that he or she should be "the sole ideas person." It is simply a myth and misconception that the innovation leader should be the source of all, or even a majority of, ideation and innovation in a business. What *is* in all of these descriptions are traits like managing, nurturing, balancing, listening, assessing, providing, etc. These are traits around the leadership and governance of innovation!

OFFICE OF INNOVATION GOVERNANCE?

Do you need an "office of innovation governance" (OIG)? My initial response would be "Not likely." Creating a separate OIG defeats and contradicts the importance and belief that innovation governance should be embedded within the business. As with anything, structures take varied forms in different organization, and an OIG may make sense in your company, especially if it is extremely large. However, I'd take caution in creating something that is seen as standalone and not integrated into the core daily business.

INNOVATION GOVERNANCE—YIN & YANG

After reading this chapter, do you see the value and synergy in having "governance" with "innovation"? When innovating in your organization, it is not sustainable, repeatable, and holistic to simply have some creativity and ideation with a few individuals. You need that execution and discipline via governance to establish some boundaries, give some guidance, and effect larger scale innovation for many people to be involved and to drive the most value. Find the right balance in your business and for your culture, but ensure you have both components of this equation to drive innovation value.

With innovation governance as the base, it's time to identify "important innovation." This isn't just about how you should evaluate innovation value in your organization—it is also for defining important innovation for your employees and other stakeholders. Knowing and understanding what is deemed important allows them to focus on innovating rather than trying to guess what leadership may or may not want.

CHAPTER 2

Determining Important Innovation

Never before in history has innovation offered promise of so much to so many in so short a time.

—Bill Gates

Most generations look at themselves in their current point in time and think, man, this is just a crazy time! We are in the midst of so much change and advancement, will it ever slow down? I do believe Bill Gates is correct, though. We are at a point in time where the world has become a very small place, a global market in which we can function quite easily, if we choose to. We have a tremendous amount of technology and information at our fingertips, with seemingly more and more coming out daily. So in this promising time, and given the importance of driving innovation in our companies, where do we start?

We shouldn't innovate for innovation's sake. What good does it do to create new products, develop new technology, file patents, and so on if you ultimately don't derive value for your customers and stakeholders? I'm not saying that every innovation project or effort has to have a 100% internal rate of return (IRR), hugely positive Net Present Value (NPV), and less than one-year payback before you do it—absolutely not! Companies need to take risks, and they need to be willing to fail when they innovate. So then how do you decide WHERE to take those risks and WHERE you should be willing to fail in order to drive value?

Before you make any decision about any innovation, you should first consider how that innovation impacts your company's overall value proposition. Consider the following examples:

- *Example*—I want to define new products and services, but only if that drives value within and fits in my value proposition.

- *Example*—I want to innovate with enabling technologies, but only where it advances my core value proposition and not just looking at technology because it is new and cool.

- *Example*—I want to innovate in my supply chain, but only where it adds value to my company's value proposition: suppliers win, customers want it and will pay for it, and we can deliver it.

Yes, innovate in all these areas. But first know your value proposition, and let the new innovation value that you ultimately create be the gut test to decide if you want to execute a specific innovation or not. To do that, consider what constitutes an "important innovation."

> *Questions should clarify, not disqualify, the innovation idea. Find ways to get to yes!*

IMPORTANT INNOVATION

Since the purpose of innovation is to create value, you want to make sure that any specific innovation you consider developing or implementing fulfills that goal. There are three essential aspects of "important innovation" that can help focus this line of evaluation:

1. Imperative, central, main, essential—*Is the idea core to your value proposition?*

2. Significant and weighty; crucial and focal—*Is it a project or idea that is big or highly leveraged?*

3. Vital, chief, key, principal—*Is it something that will take priority over other projects, and does it deserve the resources it will require?*[14]

Asking tough questions that revolve around these themes should help determine if an innovation idea or project is "important." Keep digging with clarifying questions to help peel back the layers to get at the fundamental value the innovation could provide. As you ask these questions, remember that the purpose isn't to create barriers to implementation. You want to ensure you have a full and proper understanding of the innovation. Be thorough, but also look for ways to "get to yes."

Innovation encompasses developing solutions, gaining competitive advantage, and achieving breakthrough results. However, don't get stuck thinking that all innovation must be profitable to be successful. Having a goal and mantra where all innovations need to be or will be successful is a bad approach. If that's the goal, you will never find people willing to fail and push the envelope, and failure and pushing hard are critical to innovation success. Innovate with one purpose in mind—to create more value. Sometimes this will be a more iterative process, and later innovations may drive the value. You never get to the value stage without the early trial and error.

STRATEGY MAPS DEFINE IMPORTANCE

Kaplan and Norton stress the importance of strategy articulation via a strategy map. These are a categorization of if/then causal relationships leading to value creation. Right away in the preface of their book *Strategy Maps*, Kaplan and Norton say, *"You can't manage what you can't measure, and you can't measure what you can't describe,"* pointing to the need for a strategy and a way to measure and manage it for a result. They rightly conclude that it is hard to discuss, debate, and execute a strategy that can't be articulated. A strategy map defines what is important. A strategy map is an effective evaluation tool in which to consider and evaluate innovation ideas, and it also serves as a guideline for where to innovate in the business because the important aspects of the organization have been laid out clearly and hopefully communicated to employees via the map. Your innovation roadmap should directly support the strategic imperatives that you have in the organization, and this is a way to create linkage.

You need to find a relevant way in your business to filter ideas and set boundaries, whether it's a matter of defining "what is important innovation to us" or consulting and comparing ideas against your strategy map. The more transparent you can be with employees about the filtering and evaluation process, the better the quality of ideas you will get because they understand the boundaries in which they need to innovate and what is important and valuable to the business.

> **How would you define important innovation for your organization?**

Defining important innovation for your company involves a healthy, albeit spirited, conversation with your executive team. The definition, evaluation, and filtering context may evolve over time, but it should not change completely or be modified on a frequent basis. In other words, your evaluation criteria should be tied to strategies and the strategic intent of your business, not to quarterly changes in the market place or every piece of new data that crosses your desk. Consider getting the executive team together to vet how best to define, agree to, and communicate innovation value parameters in your business. Then be sure to communicate this effectively to your teams and your workforce so you can set them up for innovation success.

YOUR DEFINITION OF IMPORTANCE

We can discuss and debate many innovation definitions. You can consider my three determining points—Core to your Value Proposition,

Big or Leverage, and Takes Priority—as guideposts in making innovation choices and investments. But the single most important element of what embodies important innovation is YOUR DEFINITION. Using other definitions and guidance is helpful, but they should always be customized and edited to make sense for your business. When I talk with businesses about innovation strategy and how they look at and judge innovation, we start with my definitions and other data points, then we edit. This may sound like a wordsmithing exercise, but it is important that the executive team be aligned on what the innovation journey should look like. And calling it a "journey" raises another important point. As you define what important innovation is at your company, keep a short-term focus and a long-term view. You may want to think about an innovation journey of three to five years, and what is important in year one may be different than years three or four. For example, in year one, you may want to evaluate and fund initiatives that have a shorter scope and higher probability of success so that you can build some momentum and early wins. Or maybe your business is in a rut and you really need to come out of the gates with a big bang and create a burning platform of change—so you launch a larger effort that focuses on a singular initiative and is not diluted with other smaller projects. So if you asked me what is the right approach on defining important innovation at your company and how to launch or relaunch your innovation journey, I'd say, "It depends."

Begin with the three points. Consider your strategy map. Look at your value proposition. Examine where your business is at from a maturity standpoint. Account for current operational issues and challenges. Think about what you've heard from your customers on your last customer visits or via feedback mechanisms. Then sketch out your three-to-five year journey as a skeletal model and focus on actions and activity to be taken in the next one to two years. Define what important innovation is to your business overall, then agree to a plan of attack on which kinds of innovation and where within your business innovation can provide the most value immediately and in the near and longer term.

"PROUDLY DISCOVERED ELSEWHERE" IDEAS

Now that you have a solid understanding of important innovation, you can use this as a test to delineate what you should or shouldn't engage in with regard to innovation within your company. What else should you be looking at with regard to your innovation viewpoints and best practices? I believe the answer is in considering ideas that are Proudly Discovered Elsewhere (PDE)—especially by looking at the products, technologies, and innovations developed by other companies, including your competitors and, more importantly, from companies outside your own industry. When you look far afield from what your company does, you may find some fascinating ideas that might be leveraged, adopted, or reinvented for your own company's use. Let me offer an illustrative story and an idea of a source where you can find PDE ideas:

> For the last several years, I have been attending the International Consumer Electronics Show (CES) in Las Vegas. This show has been going on for many years and gets bigger and bigger every year. The most recent show in 2015 was no exception. CES had 3,600 exhibitors, 2.2 million square feet of exhibitor space, 38 football fields of goodies, 170,000 participants, and 375 startup companies! One more staggering stat: CES 2015 had participants from 140 countries! That's 60% more than the 2014 Winter Olympics in Sochi! These participants and exhibitors represented a wide variety of industries and countries, but all were looking for or showcasing their latest products, technologies, and other innovations. When I was in healthcare, we had an exhibitor's booth at the conference. When I wasn't in the booth showing off our latest innovations, I and a couple of my staff would wander the floor and look at other innovations from a variety of businesses. Our goal was simple. I told them, "Go look at other innovations at the show, specifically outside of our industry, and see what innovations you could leverage, adopt, partner, or reinvent for our own use and drive more value in our healthcare business." I didn't know what we would get, but it was worth a little wandering time and creative thinking. We came back with an entire spreadsheet of ideas! Some good, some less so, but we had a lot to consider. I called those ideas, "proudly discovered elsewhere."

With PDE, it should be apparent that you don't need to create or invent "the next wheel." Sometimes you simply need to take the concept of the wheel and apply it to your industry. Given the pace of today's world, technology advancements, and globalization, there is no shortage of good ideas and innovations in existence—it really comes down to adaptation and execution!

You don't need to start from scratch. Maybe you can do a little reinvention of a concept to leapfrog the original idea or modify the innovation to make it applicable to your industry. Whether you find these ideas at a trade show, conference, event, in a book, or elsewhere, you should always be on the lookout for innovative ideas, concepts, products, and technologies that you may be able to adapt and apply to your business to better your value proposition. Learn how to redeploy, reinvent, and adapt.

OTHER QUESTIONS TO ASK

What else should you be considering to get to innovation value? Consider these questions:

1. Who can we get to help innovate?

   • Who within our business?
   • Who outside of our business?

2. How will we balance innovation projects with the other priorities we already have in play?

3. What do other companies do for innovation mechanisms or channels?

4. How should I use innovation for evaluation criteria, monitoring mechanisms, and outright measurement of value?

5. What new or additional innovation channels should we put into place, and how will they fit in with existing processes?

These are all great questions to be thinking about and asking, and the following chapters cover them in detail. Keep the concepts of "important innovation" and searching for PDE applications at the front of your mind. Remember that innovation isn't easy, but neither is it rocket science. It takes a strong leader and a thoughtful, disciplined approach to succeed. To be a leader in innovation, and specifically innovation governance, turn to Chapter 3 for what may be a surprising revelation. As a finance and accounting professional, you already possess the inherent skills needed and are well-positioned to carry out this crucial work!

CHAPTER 3

Innovation Guidance for Finance and Accounting Professionals

Excellence is an art won by training and habituation. We do not act rightly because we have virtue or excellence, but we rather have those because we have acted rightly. We are what we repeatedly do. Excellence, then, is not an act but a habit.
— Aristotle

I have been a senior finance and accounting professional and CMA® (Certified Management Accountant) since 1992. This chapter (as its title says) is intended specifically for senior finance and accounting professionals. It offers tips, warnings, and recommendations specifically from that viewpoint — accelerating how you may react (both positively and negatively) to some of the concepts and ideas of innovation and innovation governance. Consider this to be a filter on how you could approach innovation in your company — written *by* a finance and accounting professional *for* a finance and accounting professional.

If you are not a finance and accounting professional, I nevertheless encourage you to read this chapter and ask yourself, "Which of these strengths and weaknesses apply to me, and what do I need to be cognizant of in relation to leading and supporting innovation efforts? What other strengths or weaknesses should I add to these lists that also apply to me personally and professionally?"

Regardless of your professional background or position, what is important in this chapter is the traits needed to be successful in innovation leadership and management. As you'll see these strengths discussed, think about the opening quote from Aristotle. Excellence is about how we act, day in and day out — the habits that we form as leaders. Leveraging your strengths and supplementing your weaknesses with compensating tactics are important. To do so requires awareness of both.

RISK AND INNOVATION—OUR ROLE

Finance and accounting professionals often strive to protect their businesses from risk and drive it out, which is no doubt an important activity. In innovation management, however, you need to "manage" or harness risk to create value, not eliminate it. This principle may be fundamentally at odds with what you have done in the past, or it may be very natural. Whichever the case, understand this principle of managing risk to drive value. And when you think about managing risk to drive value, who better to apply that innovation governance than a strategic financial leader who already does it on a daily basis? (In Chapter 11, I'll discuss using ERM (Enterprise Risk Management) as an opportunistic avenue to get innovation ideas and value.)

CFOs can manage, support, and lead innovation through proper innovation governance, which is more than just managing risk: It extends to the entire business strategy and value creation. In addition, CFOs can help other C-suite executives innovate. Think of innovation governance as brakes on a car—not to slow the car down, but knowing you have the brakes lets you actually drive the car faster. Innovation governance provides brakes and acceleration.

I believe one reason more CFOs haven't engaged deeper in innovation is that they simply have less experience in the discipline, a lack of tools and measures that are fundamental to other things we do, and little means of a burning platform to motivate them. But we *do* have a burning platform to drive innovation, and with the tools, processes, and measures that you are about to read about and discover, I think you have the tools needed to succeed in this area!

First, let's take a closer look at Question #5 in the IMA survey to reveal how our attitudes toward innovation have changed over the years. As you read this section, keep in mind these two intents:

1. How can I leverage my inherent strengths to be a leader and supporter of innovation efforts and innovation governance?

2. Of the areas that don't come naturally to me, which might represent the inherent position of the individuals that I need to relate to, lead, and support in innovation efforts?

 The IMA survey asked respondents about the role that senior finance and accounting leaders have in innovation, how that role has evolved, and if they think it will change in the future.

When IMA asked this question, it was assumed that the role of finance professionals may have changed over time. It was surprising to see how much respondents agreed with that change! The research pointed to a very specific and dramatically sloped trend in relation to innovation and finance and accounting leaders.

- Ten years ago, 53% of respondents had little or nothing to do with leading or supporting innovation. Another 24% were only "somewhat" involved. Innovation clearly wasn't a large priority for us 10 years ago.

- Today, that 53% who had little to do with innovation has plummeted to 28%! Now, 41% are somewhat involved, and 26% are "often" involved. The pendulum has swung, and 67% of us are now supporting innovation in some fashion vs. only 47% from 10 years ago!

> **The important and difficult job is not to find the right answers, but to find the right questions.**

- Now as we look into the near future (i.e., the next 1–3 years), the pendulum will continue to swing more. That original 53% with little involvement in innovation that was cut down to 28% today will be only 17% in the near future. This research says that only one in five of us will *not* be involved in innovation! And those who are somewhat or often involved will increase again, this time from 67% to 74%, with an even larger shift for those who are "often" involved, which increases from 11% to 26% to 38% over the three time periods! That is a significant, meaningful shift.

IMA saw this as a trend before the survey, and now the research only intensified the significance as the trend continues to get larger. Senior finance and accounting professionals need to get comfortable with supporting, managing, and leading innovation in their companies. The success of our businesses and the value we bring to the market for our customers clearly depend on it. Are we ready to take on this significant—and slightly different—role from what our training and experience has prepared us for?

LEVERAGING STRENGTHS

To answer that question, let's take a look at some typical *strengths and nonstrengths* of senior finance and accounting professionals and apply those to how we can be successful in our innovation endeavors. Admittedly, the lists that follow involve stereotypes that don't apply to everyone, and there was no formal research here on the attributes of senior finance and accounting professionals. Instead, the following lists are representative of my experience, and I include them here as a starting point for your consideration of what you need to pay attention to when you are designing, implementing, and leading innovation efforts in your company.

As you read through these lists, remember the acronym ACAR, which stands for:

Awareness creates *Choices*,
Actions get *Results*.[15]

When you have an *awareness* of your strengths and weaknesses, you can make *choices*. If you aren't aware, you can't do anything! If you have choices, you can then take *actions*. If you don't take actions, you are simply aware and get little value. But if you take actions, you *will* get *results*! Having awareness, creating choices, and taking action does not guarantee perfect, great, or even good results, but I bet it will lead to successful results more often than not. So review the following lists of the perceived strengths and nonstrengths of finance and accounting professionals and consider the "how to improve" suggestions that follow.

TYPICAL NONSTRENGTHS OF SENIOR FINANCE AND ACCOUNTING PROFESSIONALS

Consider these attributes that may not be inherent skills in our finance and accounting roles, or they may be areas where we typically are not the strongest—in either case, look at ways to augment or convert these areas to strengths in supporting and leading innovation governance and leadership!

1. *We are calculating; we want data and facts—and as many as possible—before we render judgment*. Others don't worry that there are still things that are unknown. They press forward without full information. *How to change this for innovation:* Some innovation, maybe most innovation, is done with little and/or imperfect information. It can't be haphazard and careless, but it will not have a level of information that you are accustomed to having when making business decisions. Loosen up the reins in this regard when considering innovation efforts, but do so thoughtfully.

2. *We tend not to communicate passionately because we tend to use facts and figures, not enthusiastic stories*. We don't worry about marketing and hype—we tell it the way it is. *How to change this for innovation*: When you launch a new innovation program or channel, get some help from an orator who can breathe life into the communication and launch of the program. You don't have to "overcome" or "fix this weakness," just be aware of it and enlist help from your communications personnel if it's needed. Facts are always in vogue, but sometimes a little zest and enthusiasm is also required to energize and motivate others.

3. *We tend to overlook intangibles because we are looking for hard, current facts.* We tend to see reality as truth and potential as unproven facts. *How to change this for innovation*: When leading innovation efforts, keep in mind that there are tangibles and intangibles, and be quick to listen and slow to judge—not our usual mode of operation. Soliciting help from other leaders when evaluating projects and ideas is smart and can be very helpful.

4. *We tend to try to take the emotion out of the situation.* Again, we are looking for facts and truths, not emotions; there is usually enough of that in the politically charged environments we have to navigate through. *How to change this for innovation:* You should encourage people to be emotional and passionate when they are innovating, and try not to judge too quickly and jump immediately to the facts. Having said that, we do need to apply facts, judgment, and wisdom; just consider the timing and dosage when doing so.

5. *Although we budget and forecast, we typically focus on the current state* and provide recommendations and analysis on what has already happened, rather than looking to the future. And when we do look at the future, we tend to have more questions than predictions or speculations. *How to change this for innovation*: That same skill of "forensic accounting and analysis" can be deployed alternatively to be more futuristic and to analyze future opportunities. But instead of trying to be a futurist, simply find a yin to your yang and bring that person into your circle of influence.

6. *We care less about conflict and friction and more about facts*— that's our job. Although we may like harmony, that isn't our primary concern, and it can even hinder our independent view. Sometimes friction is necessary and even required. *How to change this for innovation*: Having independence and critical judgment is not the leading mantra around innovation. Evaluating results and good investments is, however, so apply your natural skills in appropriate doses.

7. *Finance and accounting leaders usually do not have the role of ideation.* We analyze and judge based on our experience and training rather than focus on the creation of things. *How to change this for innovation*: Your judgment skills will be valuable when you are looking at and evaluating ideas through multiple innovation channels. Remember, if you are leading innovation, you don't have to be (and shouldn't be) the one with all the good ideas. Even if you are in charge of leading or implementing innovation, you should focus on being the facilitator of the process and the innovation channels, not the individual who comes up with all the ideas.

8. *More than people in most functional areas, we typically deal with confidential and restricted information*. We tend to exclude rather than include others—for good reason. *How to change this for innovation*: With innovation, it's the more, the merrier! Think of ways to engage employees, customers, suppliers, and other constituents with regard to innovation. Again, look for support and help from other functional areas that are regularly engaged like this. You don't need to reinvent how to get people more involved, because others are doing it daily.

9. *We like to learn, but we tend to be deep subject matter experts in our areas*, and it's hard enough to stay up to speed in our own respective areas, much less be experts in all areas! *How to change this for innovation*: Remember what I wrote in the introduction to Part I: Innovation is a team sport. You don't need to do it alone, nor should you. You don't have to evaluate, judge, and understand all the technology or technical things that may come your way. Enable others to innovate and evaluate and fill in gaps that you need to help learn, govern, or support innovation. You should operate as the governance mechanism, not the chief ideator or chief technologist.

10. *Our work is often not popular; to a degree, we may not even care if we are liked in the organization*. Sometimes we are the score-keepers and the bad guys because we have to enforce discipline and cost control (and to a degree, self-control). *How to change this for innovation*: Think about how you can build a little more "popularity" into your innovation endeavors to win others over. Enlist others who are strong in this area for help.

TYPICAL STRENGTHS OF SENIOR FINANCE AND ACCOUNTING PROFESSIONALS

Consider how you can use these inherent strengths for innovation governance and leadership!

1. *We know how to question people and get to answers; we are very analytical*. We look for patterns. We aren't afraid to dig in. *Leverage this!* Use this strength to find value in ideas. Be analytical and dig into someone's idea to find a way to get to yes! You could very well be the turning point in deciding to take a project forward because you can see something nobody else can.

2. *We are paid to render judgment; whether popular or not, we confront the brutal facts*. It's our job, and we take control as we are required to. *Leverage this!* When considering innovative ideas and

concepts, listen first and speak second. You can and should confront innovators with questions based on your experience, but do it in a supportive manner, in a way that respectfully challenges their thinking and maybe even takes it to a higher level by peeling back a layer of the onion in a way they didn't think of. We take charge and lead everyone from the boardroom to the conference room. Help your innovators get to the next level with their ideas!

3. *We like to know the rules of the game before we jump in to play*, and sometimes we are the ones who need to enforce the rules as well. *Leverage this!* Tweak this skill during innovation endeavors to think about the "consistent opportunity" you can create for all people to innovate. If you can set the rules of the innovation game such that they are clear and concise, you should be able to better drive innovation results—you can create the right level of governance. Consistency within innovation doesn't feel like a fit to some, but I can tell you it is—consistently ask for ideas, consistently evaluate ideas.

4. *We talk about past results—duplicating good results and learning from poor results*. We create a context for the future by looking at the past. *Leverage this!* You may have distinct and deep knowledge of business operations from the various analyses you have completed and decisions you have been a part of. When new ideas are considered, don't shoot them down at face value, but ask questions based on your past experience that will challenge the innovator to ensure

> *You've climbed the ladder, now turn around and mentor someone else to a level of significance.*

the team is learning from past mistakes and can capitalize on those, thus learning for future successes and value creation.

5. *We like structure, processes, and routines*. We live in an orderly world. A world without discipline is chaos! *Leverage this!* This skill makes us excellent facilitators of innovation programs and overall governance! You can bring discipline and structure to different channels of innovation—as long as you don't over-engineer processes and make them cumbersome. Through this discipline, you also bring a level of credibility and trust from the executive leadership team and employees. Don't underestimate the level of trust that you bring to the table. Trust brings speed in getting things done, and structure and discipline can ultimately create more value in a faster timeframe!

6. *We get lots of data and information. We are filtering machines!* We have to find the needle in the haystack to make sense of things;

we are excellent at focus and filtering. *Leverage this!* Use this strong skill to give innovators focus when they come forward with ideas. Think of this in terms of a sailing analogy. When you innovate, you tend not to move straight from point A to point B. Like sailing, you tack back and forth to ultimately get to your destination. That's the iterative nature of innovation. Use this skill of focus to keep innovators within meaningful boundaries so they keep making forward progress and ultimately get to the goal.

7. ***We are repositories of information and data, and we have long memories about business successes and failures.*** We have provided and taken in a plethora of inputs. *Leverage this!* Similar to the ability to provide context, you have a lot of inherent data and information from the business—generally more than most. Leverage those inputs to help drive innovation. You may be able to provide some of these inputs in a timely fashion to actually reduce some of the iterations an innovator has to go through to build solutions. You could be a key ally to an innovator in implementing an idea and accelerating its success by sharing your knowledge and perspective!

8. ***We are often defined as responsible and reliable.*** In Maslow's Hierarchy of Needs, we have reached self-actualization when we are viewed as "trusted advisors" in our businesses. *Leverage this!* Be a trusted advisor to an innovator! Mentor innovators, as needed, on being responsible with company assets and in how to successfully provide reliable, meaningful updates to leadership. Responsibility does not mean that you can't iterate ideas and fail on occasion. You simply need to respect that which has been entrusted to you and learn to drive to a state of value. And we can encourage and teach that! You can be a strong mentor to many others and help them achieve their own self-actualization in this area.

9. ***We are professionals (CMAs, CPAs, CIAs, etc.) and want to be— need to be—credible.*** We are ethical. We want to know that we are significant and have significance (this may sound vain, but it isn't). *Leverage this!* I believe many people who thrive on innovation and being innovative thirst for significance. They want all the same things you stand for as a finance and accounting leader. Give them a taste of it, show them what credibility looks like, and mentor them to get there. When you have some level of significance in your career, turn around and look behind you on the ladder and lend a hand to help someone else so they can get up that ladder, too.

10. ***We have risen to a senior level and have become more strategic and wiser through our experiences.*** When we started as finance and accounting professionals, we had the ability to dig into the details. And many of us still enjoy digging into details to some

degree today. But we have also become strategic in leading and supporting our organizations. *Leverage this!* When you are leading or driving innovation efforts, look at the forest, not the trees. Be strategic and dive into the details when needed, but do it in a way to advance a project, not to question it, and keep others focused on the end state.

After reading through these strengths and nonstrengths, are you surprised how well-positioned you are to lead and support innovation and innovation governance in your business? It may be much closer to your comfort zone than you imagined. And it isn't a matter of "fixing" or getting better at those areas that aren't a natural fit. Rather, it's a matter of acknowledging where you may not function as well and applying compensating factors like engaging others to support, drive, and lead innovation efforts. You can do it! You are poised to lead in innovation governance, and your business needs your inherent skill sets to lead innovation governance and create innovation value!

THE CHANGING ROLE OF THE CFO—CORROBORATING EVIDENCE

Is innovation so dissimilar from other new tasks and responsibilities we are being asked to take on that are outside a CFO's traditional responsibilities? As executive and senior finance and accounting professionals, we are key players at the table who balance strategy and execution to achieve results. We have always worn many hats and participate or lead many aspects of our organization. In 2012, IMA and the Association of Chartered Certified Accountants (ACCA) teamed up on a joint research study looking at the changing role of the CFO.[16] They identified nine core areas of change:

1. Regulation—increased levels of compliance and requirements

2. Globalization—serving global clients and integrating foreign partners

3. Technology—analytics, data, and infrastructure

4. Risk—risk management and operational and strategic processes

5. Transformation—evolving the business model

6. Stakeholder management—communications and clarifications

7. Strategy—alignment, leading, managing

8. Reporting—balancing short-term and long-term priorities

9. Talent and Capability—talent development and management

If you look closely at these nine areas, you can see that innovation governance runs through them all and could be accounted for in each thematic area.

- These areas talk about new changes and challenges in our markets (globalization and technology) and how to effectively lead and govern amidst these challenges.

- They talk about a need for governance (regulation, risk, reporting), but in a balanced sense so we can make good decisions while avoiding the creation of cumbersome systems and requirements.

- They talk to strategy and evolution (transformation, stakeholder management, and strategy) and how we need to strategically evolve our organizations to be relevant, value-creating entities for our customers and stakeholders.

As we manage our talent pools and capabilities—and even plan for our own succession—we need to be diligent and broad in our thinking of the core (and evolving) skills that are needed to serve in the office of the CFO these days. As you move into the elements of creating the most effective *Innovation Elixir* for your company, keep these evolving themes and needs in mind as you consider what is needed most in your business and its environment.

ECHOING THE CALL TO ACTION

I hope that up to this point you can see and feel the urgent need for action around innovation governance and innovation value creation to improve your organization's value proposition and ultimately realize your mission and vision. Can you see that you should *and can* play a major role in innovation governance? This isn't a fad. Innovation isn't going to be an afterthought and dismissed next quarter or next year. The need for our companies to innovate around their value propositions to drive more value for customers is only going to continue to accelerate, so we had better get good at leading and managing innovation! If not us, then who?

PART II

The First Element: Galvanizing the Organization

If you're not failing every now and again, it's a sign you're not doing anything very innovative.

— Woody Allen

The first element in creating your Innovation Elixir® is about readying the organization for innovation success. In just about any important initiative you undertake as a leader, you first ask yourself, "How will the organization respond to this?" You consider the political, business, and social impacts your program will have and map the specific actions you'll need to take to ensure acceptance of your program and success as you move forward. So why is this element called "galvanizing"? Let's look to some definitions and then paint a picture of what galvanizing looks like:

Galvanization is the process of applying a protective zinc coating to steel or iron to prevent rusting. The most common method is hot-dip galvanization, in which parts are submerged in a bath of molten zinc. Galvanizing protects in two ways:

1. *It forms a coating of corrosion-resistant zinc which prevents corrosive substances from reaching the more delicate part of the metal.*

2. *The zinc serves as a sacrificial anode so that even if the coating is scratched, the exposed steel will still be protected by the remaining zinc.[17]*

Galvanizing is about strength and preparing for success. Sounds like a valuable first step to me!

CREATE A MENTAL IMAGE OF GALVANIZING

What does galvanizing look like? Think of Achilles from Greek mythology. Achilles was a Greek hero in the Trojan War. His most notable feat was the slaying of the Trojan hero Hector outside the gates of Troy. When Achilles was born, his mother Thetis tried to make him immortal by dipping him in the river Styx. However, he was left vulnerable at the part of the body by which she held him, his heel. Aside from his heel, his mother essentially "galvanized" him for protection.

Imagine "galvanizing" your business with a protective coating against things that could make it rust or deteriorate. Wouldn't it be great if you could grab your business by the heel and do a "hot-dip galvanization" to protect it? This is the picture you want to keep in mind when galvanizing your business for innovation value success—imagine a protective coating around your business to protect it from failure and ensure its win in battle!

> **Process and structure are important and, in the long term, help you gain value faster—but don't over engineer.**

From time to time, you need to galvanize your business and apply a new protective coating. Maybe the need is to protect your business from something that can hurt it, or maybe it's to ready your business for something controversial. The latter is the case in galvanizing your organization for innovation success. Galvanizing the organization for any new initiative can be tough and tricky. *Tough* because any time you launch something new, it's just that—new and unknown. It represents one more thing that the organization has to digest, implement, execute, monitor, and keep fresh. And *tricky* because something like this may have been attempted before, and the organization can have long memories of failed initiatives and a flavor-of-the-month's efforts.

As you read Chapters 4 and 5, think about how you can best ready your organization for success. What steps can you take to inform your employees and empower them to contribute and thrive? And, ultimately, how can your business capitalize on an innovation focus?

How will you know when you have properly galvanized the organization? You have partially galvanized your business and employees when they tell you and other executives what they really think—in a positive manner without fear of retaliation or immediate judgment. This is a solid start down the right path.

Be sure you are ready for and communicate that *failure is okay and acceptable*. It's one thing to say it, but it's another (much harder) thing to do when real dollars are at risk and other priorities are put on hold to test innovation concepts and execute speculative projects. Be sure you are ready for this journey and can back up the words because nothing shuts down innovation ideas and risk taking by your employees faster than punishing or chastising people for failure.

This section lays a foundation. It talks about the importance of understanding cultural differences in your particular organization and creating linkages with existing business processes. As you build this foundation, always be cognizant of how you can create staying power and longevity for anything you implement. Many times longevity is achieved by forming strong linkages with other constituents and business processes. Your foundation also needs clarity about what innovation is and what is going to get attention and resourced in your organization. Don't make it a secret code to crack. Make it painfully obvious the types of innovation you desire in your business, then stand back. Let's begin that foundation!

CHAPTER 4

The Foundation: Linking Innovation to Business Practices

I have not failed. I've just found 10,000 ways that won't work.

—Thomas Edison

How can you not start the foundation of our innovation journey with a quote from Thomas Edison?! Keep this quote—and the spirit of Thomas Edison—at the back of your mind (if not the front) while you begin to set an innovation foundation. Take a deep breath, heave a sigh if needed, and then get started!

When I give a lecture or workshop on business strategy, I often show two pictures at the beginning of the discussion. The first is a picture of a chess board. I talk about how many people think strategy is a lofty head game that requires planning 10 moves ahead to ensure success. While planning ahead is important, there is something even more important. And that's when I show the second picture—a picture of a rugby team in a scrum.

Get into the game and make a play! You can't win by sitting on the sideline and planning what you are going to do. You shouldn't be careless and reckless, but at some point you need to get into the scrum, make a play for better or worse, and get going. The same can be said for innovation and driving ideation and experimentation—lead and support others to get in the game and take action!

From an organizational standpoint, start with your innovation initiative at the top of the hierarchy. Although it is practically a cliché at this point that any kind of project or initiative needs to start at the top to be successful, it is certainly true with innovation. If you have the type of CEO who is uncomfortable with failure and unwilling to experiment, you may have an issue.

That isn't to say you should be comfortable and embrace large levels of failure, but you have to be willing to push the edge of the envelope, test many new ideas and concepts, and accept a certain percentage of failure when you innovate. I'd simply run by this rule and try to emulate Edison's mantra:

If you are going to fail, fail fast! Move forward and apply that learning and don't repeat it.

LINKING INNOVATION TO EXISTING BUSINESS PROCESSES

As you plan your basis for an innovation program, you should think immediately about how you can ensure that your innovation efforts and programs will last for more than a quarter or a year. We've all seen programs come and go with little, if any, value accrued. So when you set up your innovation program, processes, and channels, do this one simple but often overlooked thing: *Tie your innovation design, execution, and reporting to existing business processes!*

Many times, managers try to create innovation programs as a separate entity, separate space, or separate discussion, which can be a mistake. Why only innovate in a specific area, with a few individuals and a few dollars? Innovate across the entire business, in all spaces, and with all resources! To make innovation a part of your organization's DNA, it needs to be part of the existing, routine business processes. That gives it staying power, doesn't require a special meeting, area, or individual, and ensures it is considered in *everything* already being doing in your business—especially in areas focused on execution.

Consider the following common business processes and how you can tie innovation discussion and focus into each of these existing business processes:

Linking Innovation to Capital Allocation/Management

This is the easiest, most natural link to innovation. How much of your capital plan is allocated to innovation projects and product innovations? Consider the amount of time you already spend talking about capital investments, reviewing them, and debating resource allocations and investment returns. Why not simply tweak some of this conversation to talk about how to best invest in your business to maximize your value proposition and customer value creation through a balance of innovation projects?

Linking Innovation to Business/Strategic Planning

This is another easy fit with innovation. As you evaluate turbulence in your market, assess customer needs, review your value proposition, and assess core competencies. In what areas do you need to innovate or reinvent products or processes? Have you ever seen a strategic business plan that doesn't address innovation in one way or another? You can't just *talk* about being innovative. You need to show how you plan to innovate:

- How will you incrementally improve your existing operations?

- How will you distinguish or differentiate your value proposition to your market against your competitors?

- How will you take calculated "big bets" on breakthrough areas of your business (product, technology, partnerships, markets, etc.) without risking your entire core business?

Answer these questions and keep planning and executing your strategy. You'll soon be leading the pack.

Linking Innovation to Budgeting

Depending on your role in the organization, budgeting is either a key process or a necessary evil. Either way, make it better by introducing some innovation discussion within the budget review processes and cycles. You already challenge functional leaders and mid-level managers to be responsible for budgets and create operating plans for the year. Do they allow for unexpected surprises and opportunities where they could innovate? Will they have resources to respond to opportunities and execute on innovation improvements or big ideas? What is the mechanism to handle unfunded opportunities? You either need to account for some reserve funds to deal with unfunded opportunities, or you need to hold individual departments accountable to work on this on their own.

Unfortunately, the default I've seen is, "We don't have a budget for this good idea, so we'll have to table it until next year." Generally, small companies are more nimble than this and can respond to ideas faster. Make sure you are ready to handle, fund, and execute good ideas that come up after planning and budgeting. If you are at a larger company, you need to find a way to work in your environment so that it is possible to move swiftly to fund and execute ideas that arise in the midst of a budget cycle. Then you will be ready when the next cycle begins.

Linking Innovation to Operations Management

Almost all companies have one flavor or another of this management process. Most companies have a monthly operations review (or "ops review"), which typically reviews the results of the prior month, including financials, operational delivery and quality, and progress against strategic projects and initiatives. There are a couple of reasons to tie innovation and innovation discussion into an ops review. Operations people are in a constant state of problem solving to drive results. They are some of the best problem-solving people you will find in your organization. They must execute on a daily fashion to deliver to customers. Why not tap into that skill set to drive companywide innovation? Many times some of your best incremental and distinctive innovation ideas come from front-line people who are in operations or out in front of customers on a daily basis. When you are in an operations review session, simply ask some questions around innovation.

Improving current operations may not be the path to that special, sexy breakthrough innovation that leaders and markets like to see and write about, but it is fundamental to business success. Call it continuous improvement if you want, but just do it! Anytime you are improving your operations—improving how you execute and deliver on your value proposition to your customers—you are innovating

THE WHEEL HAS BEEN INVENTED!

Yes, some innovation is breakthrough and invents a "new wheel," but many innovations already exist in other companies, industries, and applications. Find ways to learn about innovations/reinventions in places outside your company and apply them to your business. I mentioned Proudly Discovered Elsewhere ideas in Chapter 2. Give this serious consideration. Even if you didn't achieve any new or breakthrough innovation in your entire business career, you could take other innovation achievements, processes, business models, and technology from other industries and apply them to your business and industry. Consider the innovation or invention of the following items and what others did to create value in their own businesses. What could you be doing?

> *Learn about innovation and reinventions in places outside your company, and apply them to yours!*

- *New business models*, e.g., subscription service model. A subscription model for software was once unheard of; now much of the software we use and need is sold via a subscription service. Could one of your products or services utilize a subscription model that your clients would prefer over a more standard economic model?

- *New manufacturing techniques*, e.g., 3D printing and speed of prototyping. 3D printers have been around a while, but only recently have they really come to the mass market. 3D printing techniques are enabling many businesses to do many things and with greater speed and accuracy—not just prototyping.

- *New markets and how you can get into those value chains*, e.g., SEO (search engine optimization) solutions. Are you using SEO techniques to mine for customers and market insights? New market niches seem to form almost daily—how are you learning about these market niches, and are you effectively marketing to them?

- *New products*, e.g., drones. Think about new products that get launched, like the recent surge of drones. Find a practical use for drones in your business, or somehow find a niche in that value chain for your business to support. Think of other products that are surging and how you could play a part in their value chain.

Always be on the lookout for other innovations or ideas that you could leverage, adopt, partner, or reinvent for your own use and drive more value in your business. Be on the watch for PDE opportunities!

Do your core values share your desire and need to innovate and drive innovation in the business activities that you execute? If yes, that's great! If you are unsure, you may want to add or modify your stated values to include something that shows you support for and desire to innovate. Ensure you promote the importance of collaboration, problem solving (independently and as a team), technology utilization, challenging the status quo, and the experimentation that is enormously easier today with rapid prototyping in design and social media for market testing. All of these are things that make innovation thrive.

IMPLEMENTING REWARDS SYSTEMS

Anytime you ask employees or stakeholders for ideas, contributions, or simply to spend their time on something, you need to think about compensation or ways of rewarding for results. Keep in mind that not everything is about monetary gain! You'll absolutely find people who will be motivated by money, bonuses, raises, or incentives to innovate, improve, and drive value—no doubt. But don't underestimate the value of other simple incentives, such as a thank you, recognition among their peers, recognition in a company newsletter, or other simple, nominal expressions and rewards. One of the best stories I can offer you is the following.

We had a particular business challenge for the month in our segment. It was a team challenge, so we asked teams to come up with solutions to a business challenge that we had outlined for them. We gave employees parameters of a real problem we were facing, and people were to gather in teams of five to come up with ideas for a solution and lay out an implementation plan. We had several meaningful, thoughtful, and articulate responses. We settled on a winner and implemented their solution.

As recognition, we had this team of five come to our monthly executive team meeting, which included the top 24 executives in the business. We asked the innovation team to take 10 minutes and share their solution with the entire leadership team and talk about their experience. It was a simple verbal update—no PowerPoint slides—and the team got a rousing ovation from the entire executive team when they were done. I thought a couple of the team members were going to cry with tears of joy! As I escorted them out the door and thanked them for coming to the executive team meeting and sharing, one individual, interestingly enough, an actuary, told me the following:

"That was amazing! I felt like such a rock star! I know how hard it is to get any executive time and to have the entire executive team listening to what we did, how we took a real business problem and solved it, and then get applauded like that—I just simply felt like a rock star. I can't wait to go back and tell my team."

That actuary was a rock star. He and his teammates nailed it. They took a business problem and innovated a solution. Their only reward was 10 minutes of recognition in front of their leaders, which they normally wouldn't get, and some simple applause. That reward was pure gold.

Don't reengineer the world of compensation mechanisms when considering rewards. Yes, do think of ways to offer some monetary rewards for innovation success, but also think of the simple things that have longer and more lasting impact.

COMMUNICATING INNOVATION EFFORTS AND RESULTS

This leads me to one final foundational element required for innovation success in your firm. Consider how you will communicate innovation results and the status of projects. Get your marketing, human resources, public relations, and investor relations teams involved. There is a role for all of them!

First consider what innovation results and progress you want to share internally vs. externally. For external sharing, think about when you will be ready to sell new products or implement new procedures in your business so as not to overpromise the market and set unrealistic expectations. Also think about a structured, continuous release of innovation results and progress experientially. Think about what you can release to the market on a quarterly and annual basis, not just a one time or random event. Think of continuous innovation releases and creating excitement in the market.

Internal communications around innovation should be similar. Consider different ways of communicating innovation results: during existing mechanisms like operation reviews, shout-outs on wins during a town hall meeting, a text to all employees on a win, and so on. But also be sure to communicate failures: failed ideas or implementations (not individuals) and what was learned from those failures. Celebrate wins *and* attempts. Show and communicate it all.

GALVANIZED FOR INNOVATION READINESS—YES OR NO?

How do you know when your organization has been galvanized for innovation success? There is a template in the Appendix (Innovation Foundation Readiness Checklist) that will give you a test for innovation readiness; in addition, here are some other intangible indicators that show how people in a healthy company culture can be very accepting of ideas:

- *You notice a drastic increase in the number of possible ideas you have to choose from when you enter the next idea generation process.*

- *You and your employees gain insight into how far you can stretch your own comfort zones and how open minded you have become.*

- *You experience the "Jiffy Pop" syndrome in which ideas are produced faster than you can even record them.*

- *You hear your employees make comments about how it seems they are receiving more respect.*

- *You are surprised by the idea output from even your most shy or introverted team members.*[18]

If you start seeing these elements at work, you have created a healthy culture where innovation is respected and expected. Take a look at the Checklist in the Appendix for a more comprehensive readiness assessment.

You can't start to accrue innovation value until you start to execute. Get to execution as fast as you can, but take the proper time and steps to galvanize your organization first. All that execution may fall on deaf ears and be for naught if people are not ready, willing, and able to foster, lead, support, and drive innovation efforts.

CHAPTER 5

Defining Innovation—A Balanced Approach

I am looking for a lot of people who have an infinite capacity to not know what can't be done.

—Henry Ford

How you look at innovation, describe it, and characterize it is important. You should create a lexicon, an innovation vernacular that all employees can understand and use. Think of the book *StrengthsFinder,* which created a lexicon of 34 strengths with associated definitions. When someone reads that book and takes the test to find their strengths, they can easily compare and contrast what they consider their strengths, their teams' strengths, and so on. And it isn't just a lexicon, it establishes some rules of the road. You can—and should—do the same with innovation: Describe small and large innovations, what is expected, what is accepted in your organization, and how it gets executed.

I used a balanced approach to innovation at companies. Consider a baseball analogy. Good defense and great pitching are crucial to winning a baseball game. But at the end of the day, if you don't score any runs, you have zero chance of winning. Therefore, scoring runs is important to win. What is the best way to score runs? Well, that depends. Baseball is about situations, players, matchups, and many extraneous factors. In an oversimplified summary, I'd suggest you need to hit singles along with extra-base hits (doubles, triples, and home runs) in order to score runs to win the game. I don't think it's the best strategy to just hit singles, and swinging for the fences on every at bat is going to produce a low probability of consistently winning games. Therefore, to win in baseball, you need a balanced offensive attack—you need to hit singles, doubles, triples, *and* home runs to win.

Succeeding at innovation in your business is the same as that offensive baseball strategy. You need to innovate across your business such that you get small, medium, and large results by taking on small, medium, and large initiatives and risks to get the associated payoffs.

Instead of thinking in terms of small, medium, and large, however, think in terms of *Incremental, Distinctive,* and *Breakthrough* efforts. These are the three buckets to stratify your innovation efforts.

> **Have an innovation program that solicits, evaluates, and implements a blend of innovation ideas.**

Why limit innovation to just the big ideas? Smaller ideas and innovations can add up in a hurry, more people can be involved in them, and they are often faster to implement. So don't waste time nit-picking where something should be classified as truly being innovative or not; instead, focus on innovating!

These three buckets of innovation also lead to a balanced portfolio view (not necessarily equal, but a diverse range) of innovation within your company. Just like you have a product portfolio with new products, mature products, products in decline, and so on, you should have varied degrees of innovation that support and improve your business's strategy. In business, you may not be ready for a breakthrough product. Maybe you need some incremental innovation on existing programs. Maybe you are having a hard time differentiating your offerings from competitors, so you need some distinctive advances. One of the best ways to have continuous and consistent innovation success is to have an innovation program and mindset that solicits, evaluates, and implements a blend of innovation projects and ideas—Incremental, Distinctive, and Breakthrough ideas.

INCREMENTAL INNOVATION

Staying with the baseball analogy, incremental innovation is akin to hitting a single in baseball. This type of innovation isn't about swinging for the fence and getting it all at once; it's about looking at the larger game, getting a hit, and moving someone into scoring position. You could call incremental innovation a continuous process improvement if you wanted to, but I think that is irrelevant. I only care about driving improvements in the business—improvements that further your value proposition so that you can execute better, cheaper, and faster for your customers.

Incremental innovation is also something that everyone in your business should be doing. The following line should be in every person's job description:

> "Along with the other roles and responsibilities of this position, this role requires an individual who will constantly challenge the status quo and look for ways to innovate products and processes to drive value for our customers."

Shouldn't that be the last line, or maybe the first line, of every job description? Empower staff to be responsible to look for improvements. Tell them that it's more than just okay—you expect them to do that.

EXAMPLES OF INCREMENTAL INNOVATION

Consider incremental improvement via phone apps. Think about what it's like when you download a great app on your phone. You tell everyone about the app and how it helps you with something. But inevitably, there can be a little snag or glitch that irritates you or could simply be better.

If you're lucky, a couple weeks go by and all of a sudden, there is an updated version available for download! Someone has found or heard about the improvement opportunity or somehow made the app better. You download the latest and greatest version of your beloved app and are a happy camper again. Your experience and satisfaction have changed you from being enthusiastic to a raving fan!

Incremental innovation doesn't have to be huge, but it has to be impactful and can often lead to improved customer satisfaction and retention because customers see that you care about what they have currently compared to spending all your time creating the next big thing.

When you consider roles in your organization around incremental innovation, the classic role of the industrial engineer comes to mind. Industrial engineers can certainly have big and distinctive ideas, but many times their role is to look at existing operations and find ways to incrementally improve the operation to get more, faster, better, cheaper results, thus adding significant value. They may partner with design engineers to reengineer a machine or process, but their core role is normally around incremental improvement. Think about how you can be an industrial engineer in your business and promote others to think to improve every day results.

Measuring Incremental Innovation

There will be a full discussion on measuring innovation in Part IV, but here are three metrics for context in this area. I would recommend specifically monitoring these three metrics to assess the health of your improvement efforts and, ultimately, your overall business health in relation to incremental innovation.

1. *Customer Satisfaction*—Your customers will be more satisfied with incremental improvements to products and services they have already bought. You are creating an even bigger following by driving customer satisfaction through incremental innovation. In contrast, if your customer satisfaction is low, what can you do through incremental innovation to raise your customer satisfaction levels?

2. *Customer Retention*—Happy customers are retained customers. If your retention is poor, you are attracting clients and losing them

in execution. It may be time to do some incremental innovation in what you deliver to them so that you can make them happy customers who stick around.

3. *On Time Delivery (OTD) and Quality*—Incremental improvements must always be sought in how you execute on today's value proposition to your customers. Unless your OTD is at 100% and your quality defect rate and returns at zero, you can always improve.

Incremental Innovation Key Takeaway

It is unlikely that incremental innovation will produce headlines in *The Wall Street Journal*, but incremental innovation should have the safest and most consistent return on investment since it involves the least risk and should be the most straightforward to implement. This is also the category that just about any and every employee, should be able to participate in regardless of skill set or position. Every employee should be looking for small innovations that drive value to customers. They add up quickly, and your customers will become even bigger advocates for you!

DISTINCTIVE INNOVATION

If incremental innovation is a single, distinctive innovation would be a double or a triple in baseball. You are swinging a little harder at the plate, you are taking a little more risk as you round the bases. And with this increased risk comes increased potential reward.

In my view, distinctive innovation is something that helps you differentiate your value proposition from your competitors. Traditionally, a distinctive innovation leverages existing assets and core competencies to create or offer something different in your value proposition vs. your competition. It isn't an incremental improvement making something better or cheaper to produce. It is making your product or service different—such that your customers are willing to pay more money for it now because that they see it as differentiated in the market.

Many times, distinctive innovation will require capital resources and more time to implement. As a matter of fact, take a hard look at your capital process and what is on your list for capital investment over the next year in regard to the discretionary spending. Along with the "keep the lights on" operational investments you need to make, are you spending your limited capital resources on something that will help differentiate you in the market? Shouldn't differentiation be a hurdle to make your capital list?

In many ways, distinctive innovation can be about core competencies. What are your company's core competencies, and how do you differentiate in a world of ever-increasing commoditization of products and services? Is what you are doing around distinctive innovation something that you should consider a product/process patent for? Not everything needs intellectual property (IP) protection, but if you are truly distinctive in your innovation, this is a valid question. If the IP question is a quick "no," it's likely not a distinctive innovation. But if you do believe that the idea warrants the potential for IP protection, whether you take that action or not, now you are on the right track to do something distinctive and differentiating.

Examples of Distinctive Innovation

Distinctive innovation examples can be thought of as "evolutionary" progress and changes to your value proposition rather than "revolutionary" changes.

A couple of decades ago, Hertz was clearly the dominating car rental company. It was easily evidenced by the long lines at the Hertz counter vs. the lines at Avis, National, Alamo, and so on. But success created a problem for Hertz and an opportunity for its competitors. The lines were long because customers wanted Hertz, but it took customers a while to get through the line to actually pick up their car. Frustrated, they started going to competitors so that they could get their car faster and get on with their business or pleasure time.

At some point, Hertz recognized this risk and countered with a distinctive offering. It put in place something called the Gold Club. That doesn't seem distinctive today, but it certainly was at the time. Hertz won its customers back because it touted a service and system that kept customers from having to stand in line to get a car; instead, they were expedited through the line. And eventually the company introduced the reader boards that show the car's parking spot next to the customer's name, so people didn't need to go in any line or talk with anyone when they arrived!

Hertz took a competitive disadvantage and turned it into a differentiator! It didn't take Hertz's competitors long to follow suit with the Gold Club concept, but Hertz certainly won as a first mover of this concept.

This is a classic example of an innovation that was clearly more than incremental, but not revolutionary or breakthrough. It could best be described as a modification to their value proposition that created value to their customers.

Measuring Distinctive Innovation

Consider these three metrics to measure distinctive innovation:

1. *The Number of New Products, Reinventions, or Markets*—As mentioned in the introduction, the new rule of thumb for reinventing your business is only a five-year period. Those that are stagnant won't have staying power in the long term, and those that create new products, enter new markets, or at least reinvent and improve their existing products and services will survive and thrive.

2. *The Number of New Customers*—You need to take care of your existing customers and retain them, but innovative companies that are growing through value creation are finding ways of reaching more and new customers.

3. *Net Promoter Score (NPS)*—Simply track the answer to the NPS question *"How likely are you to recommend our company/product/ service to your friends and colleagues?"* If you are engaging in, executing, and delivering distinctive innovation, you will likely have a high NPS score, a happy and growing customer base, and, therefore, are delivering and creating value in the overall market.

Distinctive Innovation Key Takeaway

Regardless of how you split your resources to drive innovation across the three types of innovation, I believe that the majority of businesses should have a disproportionate amount of resources dedicated to distinctive innovation.

> *How do you currently allocate/ balance your resources on innovation projects?*

Why? Because incremental is good and the least risky, but it takes a lot of incremental innovation to add up. Breakthrough innovation is the opposite. It can take a lot of investment and be very risky—sometimes paying off, sometimes not. Therefore, the takeaway here is to consider a disproportionate spending of resources on distinctive innovation, at least as a starting point. This type of innovation should best support, enhance, and drive your value proposition in the market and balance your needs for innovation with your risk appetite.

BREAKTHROUGH INNOVATION

When people talk about innovation, this is what many people think of. It's swinging for the fences, for the home run that defines a game or a career.

Breakthrough innovations are the most spectacular of innovations, but they are also the least frequent, carry the most risk, and usually require a large bet of resources or time. That isn't to say you shouldn't be swinging for a home run at times, but just not every time you step up to the plate.

When considering breakthrough innovation, look to do something that really doesn't exist in your industry, or look to create a new market or a new category of product that doesn't exist today. A classic example of this is the creation of *Cirque du Soleil*, which was a reinvention of the circus. Look at the new market *Cirque du Soleil* created and the success that it has generated. More modern examples that continue to play out today include Amazon in distribution (of just about everything now, including groceries) and Facebook starting a social media wave that seems to change weekly with new technologies and consumer habits.

Where do you get these breakthrough ideas? Customer feedback is always a great place for valuable ideas. If you follow a sound business process of asking your customers what they want and deliver on that, you are likely quite successful.

But in breakthrough innovation, customers often can't articulate what they may want in the future because the future can be so different from what they have today. Think of what the Internet did for distribution or what the iPhone did for the customer experience of mobile devices. No customers asked for these because they didn't know they were possible! These inventions were breakthrough and disruptive innovations. They defined new categories, created new markets, and many times made old products/markets obsolete. Most executive market leaders in business (at least the good ones) spend a percentage of time looking for breakthrough innovations and how they can redefine or reinvent their company's products and their market space.

Breakthrough innovation is risky and takes resources. It also requires some commitment and guts to look at regularly. Two keys are to have balance and discipline: *balance* to not cut this activity when there are short-term pressures on your P&L and *discipline* to keep from having too many breakthrough innovation concepts in the pipeline at once so that you end up unnecessarily betting the farm of your core business on too many wild ideas.

Examples of Breakthrough Innovation

Here are breakthrough examples from throughout history:

1. *The Model T assembly line in the early 1900s.* The assembly line developed for the Ford Model T began operation on December 1, 1913, changing manufacturing forever...

2. *MRI (magnetic resonance imaging) machines in the 1970s.* A medical imaging technique used in radiology to investigate the anatomy and function of the body in both health and disease, the MRI changed how we examined patients forever...

3. *3D printers today.* 3D printers surfaced in the 1980s but have gotten a lot more advanced and exposure in our current decade. Additive manufacturing or 3D printing is a process of making a three-dimensional solid object of virtually any shape from a digital model. Time will tell on the impacts, but it certainly appears to be breakthrough.

Measuring Breakthrough Innovation

How could you measure and monitor breakthrough innovation? Consider these metrics:

1. *New Business Revenue from New Markets*—Think 3M. It looks at new business revenue defined by sales from products introduced during the last three years. Although new products may be considered more distinctive, I believe that entering new markets can be considered more breakthrough. Either way, it's a metric to monitor innovation health.

2. *Breakthrough Innovation Funnel*—Measure your intake of breakthrough ideas, how many pass the first gate of evaluation and are researched, how many are implemented, and how many succeed. To get results at the end of the funnel, you need to calculate the proper intake of ideas to begin with.

3. *Third-Party Validations*—If you are getting recognition via awards and articles for what you are doing via breakthrough innovations, you are doing something that is likely extraordinary because it is getting recognized by people outside your industry and market, creating larger mainstream buzz.

Do you have any breakthrough innovations in your pipeline? If you don't invent or reinvent the future, somebody else will! While you don't want to focus all your time and resources on breakthrough innovations, you certainly do want to have a couple of breakthrough innovation projects in your portfolio that you are working on.

 Where do you allocate your resources? On what types of innovation? I started this chapter saying that you need to have a "balance" of innovation in your portfolio, a balance across the three buckets: incremental, distinctive, and breakthrough.

But *balance* doesn't mean *equal*! So the key concern is how to split your innovation resources and time across these three areas? Exhibit 5-1 shows what the IMA respondents said.

Incremental	Distinctive	Breakthrough
Exhibit 5-1: How Respondents Balance Their Resources		
Incremental	*Distinctive*	*Breakthrough*
6% respondents said 0%	6% said 0%	12% said 0%
23% respondents said 50%	21% said 30%	24% said 20%
80% responded <51%	**60% said 30–50%**	**46% said 20–30%**
2% respondents said 100%	0% said 100%	0% said 100%

Extremes of spending (0% or 100% of your resources) in one of the three buckets was limited. That's good and holds with the principle of having some balance. Incremental tended to be the bucket that most people would put their resources in, followed by distinctive and then breakthrough.

This underscores the pressures of managing current goals and financial expectations. In some industries and business models, shifting more resources from incremental to distinctive will help to add more value to your overall value proposition. If you go back to the idea that you need to be reinventing your value proposition every five years, then you can't reinvent your value proposition when 50% or more of your innovation efforts are focused on incremental initiatives. You need to think bigger.

Having said that, exercise prudence and don't put too much into the breakthrough area. Survey respondents show that it was important to have a meaningful mix in this area, but it was the smallest bucket—likely due to the associated risk.

Ultimately, there is no singular correct allocation among the three categories except for the need to be thoughtful and intentional—that is, have your eyes wide open as to where you are spending your innovation dollars and time, and make sure that mirrors the needs of your value proposition reinvention and overall business goals.

MEASURING INNOVATION VALUE

It's important to begin to consider how to measure innovation value, especially in Part III on *Enabling*. IMA asked respondents how they measure innovation success and value today. They said:

- 16% use the number of new products, services, and/or patents

- 14% use the percentage of sales revenue from new products

- 8% use customer retention

- 4% use something else

- 58% said "We don't formally measure innovation success/value"

Wow! 58% of respondents don't formally measure innovation success or value. Based on other parts of the survey, I interpolate the root of that answer to come from the fact that innovation is hard to measure. This is something Part IV can help with.

It's critical to find more and better ways to measure innovation—not to perfectly calculate value and success, but to establish a baseline and stride for marked improvement in your innovation journey and efforts. You have to be able to measure to show improvement and know that you are driving more value in your business.

BUSINESS MODEL INNOVATION

Breakthrough innovations can lead to full-scale business model innovation. Business model innovation can be addressed as a breakthrough project, but sometimes it can go beyond that and needs to be handled with kid gloves. Business model innovation is needed when companies like Uber or Google or Amazon enter and upend your industry. There can also be changes in the economic models in your business, as is happening with healthcare today. Target custom models and demographics can also shift with direct selling, using brokers, as well as new interest from rising economies and new geographic interest.

Business model innovation is important innovation, but unlike much of what we'll talk about in this book, that type of innovation is mostly done by a handful of people behind tightly closed doors. Why? Because of the sheer nature of the disruption to the business. It's difficult to talk to current employees about how to entirely change your value proposition and changing the daily way that you execute to deliver. That can be a very scary thing and not something you want to broadcast very widely. I want to acknowledge this type of innovation, and it certainly is important and strategic, but it is not a process or channel in which you would engage very many people.

CLOSING THOUGHT

Innovation can and should come from all types of people, and you know you want innovation at all levels—small, medium, and large. Go back to the quote at the beginning of this chapter from Henry Ford: "*I am looking for a lot of people who have an infinite capacity to not know what can't be done.*" You should facilitate innovation in your organization such that you have a plethora of people who are willing to ignore the status quo and innovate new products, processes, and ways to create value at all levels.

Galvanize your organization for innovation—ready them by being clear in intent and having a culture that supports and rewards innovation. Communicate your innovation results internally and externally as it makes sense. "*Begin with the end in mind*" as Stephen Covey would say, then turn your workforce loose!

ACTION: Before proceeding to the next chapter, use the following form as a worksheet to reflect on Chapters 4 & 5, the first element of your innovation elixir. What were your key takeaways from this chapter, and how will you customize these tools and principles to drive value in your company? Don't wait until the end of the book. Begin formulating your innovation elixir now!

replace with LOGO

GOLD NUGGETS
APPLICATION AT MY BUSINESS

THREE Gold Nuggets you are taking away as foundational elements of your innovation strategy, items for discussion and contemplation at your business with your teams, or concepts that need further research: *(circle one)*

1. *FOUNDATIONAL / DISCUSS / RESEARCH* _____

2. *FOUNDATIONAL / DISCUSS / RESEARCH* _____

3. *FOUNDATIONAL / DISCUSS / RESEARCH* _____

Concept to Execution → which concepts will I implement at our business?

Implement Immediately:	Reserve/Consider Later
A. _____	C. _____
B. _____	D. _____

Innovation Elixir – The Secret Potion at My Business.

What specific tweaks would I need to make to achieve success at my business, with its unique culture, employees & leadership?

1. _____

2. _____

3. _____

PART III

The Second Element: Enabling Innovation—Innovation Processes and Channels

If you always do what you always did, you will always get what you always got.

—Albert Einstein

How can I not acknowledge Albert Einstein in a book discussing innovation? This is one of my favorite quotes of his, and it applies to the second element in the Innovation Elixir. There are multiple ways for you to *enable* innovation in your company. This section of the book examines five specific channels or mechanisms you can consider and implement to collect, evaluate, and harvest innovation value. If you simply talk about innovation without changing the way you do things, you *"will get what you always got."* Setting up these processes and channels is important.

Simply put, how are you going to get your employees and other stakeholders to innovate? You don't just show up for work one day and say, "Okay, we are now going to be an innovative company. Ready, set, innovate!" You're a leader, right? So this is where you need to lead.

Set up your organization for success by putting in multiple innovation channels. A channel is simply a way in which you will *solicit, collect, evaluate, design, implement*, and *monitor* innovation activity. Why do you need multiple innovation channels? Because businesses, industries, companies, employees, and leadership are different. They are in different stages of business maturity and deal with different turbulences.

Think of a product life-cycle curve. Companies have a different mix of products/services and different risk profiles, even within the same company. Different channels are needed to capture and implement innovations from all areas of a business. The APQC's (American Productivity & Quality Center) top 10 best practices in innovation states that you should *"Drive innovation from the top and bottom."* Leadership support is essential, and the leaders in any organization need to provide resources and support so that innovators can be successful. They can also lead innovation from the top by how they set up business challenges and future sensing groups.

However, some channels need to be "bottom up" and let innovation be a grassroots effort. Therefore, you need channels that work as top-down channels and channels that can be grass roots.

> **Are you leaving innovation value on the table simply because you haven't asked for input?**

As you read about the five innovation channels to *enable* your organization, realize that all may not fit in your industry, business, or culture at a given point of time. Therefore, think about the following factors:

- Which of these will work in your organization?
- When would be the most appropriate time to introduce them?
- How can they be specifically modified to get maximum results in your business?

In general, best practices are good to learn from, but some adaptation is normally required to achieve the most and best success.

WHERE DO YOU GET INNOVATION IDEAS?

This section focuses on *where* and *how* to solicit, review, evaluate, implement, and monitor innovation ideas and projects. In a webinar I conducted on "Business Strategy and Innovation" for Proformative, an organization that provides learning and continuing professional education (CPE) opportunities for senior finance professionals, I asked the 175 participants the following question, and the percentages here represent the final poll results:

What is your company's biggest source of innovation?

a.	*One or two critical thinkers*	*30%*
b.	*Internal employees suggestions/programs*	*29%*
c.	*Client feedback/input*	*25%*
d.	*Fast follower strategy to competitors*	*10%*
e.	*N/A*	*6%*

The results were not surprising, but validating and a little concerning. The good news is that 29% had internal employee suggestions or programs to solicit ideas, and 25% are asking their customers—a good start! But what are the other 71% to 75% of companies doing if they aren't even asking their employees and customers?

The bad news is that the highest rated answer at 30% was "One or two critical thinkers." What happens when that critical thinker or two is no longer around? Proper innovation governance would never tie all or even a majority of your innovation ideation to one or two individuals. As a senior leader in the business, you need to find ways to foster innovation ideation for many constituents. This should be your focus, and it's why the next chapters explore implementing multiple innovation channels.

I respect the 10% who have adopted a fast follower strategy—that can be a smart thing to do from time to time when you don't want to be on the leading edge (or bleeding edge) but want to move quickly to follow your competition and with normally less risk and investment. But I would argue that you can't regularly make that a habit. Although it is a smart strategy or channel in some circumstances, it can't be your only approach.

Another research data point on innovation sources comes from the IMA research. Respondents were asked about the source for ideas today and where they would like to get ideas from. The responses were not totally surprising—but they confirmed that these are good sources of ideation for some and a clear opportunity for others to use:

- 57% said key employees who are charged with innovation and ideation
- 52% said employees via idea suggestions
- 43% said customers
- 41% said external agencies/consultants/institutions
- 36% said competitors (i.e., the "fast follower" strategy)
- 31% said key suppliers

The fact that the highest channel of innovation (57%) is using a handful of key employees is not surprising and similar to the Proformative polling. Consider if you want your value proposition and core business strategy linked to one or two people or to a much larger group of employees?

I would vote for the latter. Having a single point of failure is just not smart planning and strategy.

Fifty-two percent of respondents get ideas from employees via some sort of suggestion process. This is great, but why are the other 48% of companies not asking their employees? Would you feel valued if you were an employee in one of those companies? Probably not. This channel is ripe for the other 48% to start doing something.

As you look at the remaining channels, the question is simple: Why are you not asking these constituents to provide suggestions and value to improve and grow your company? Many of them want to help you because if you are successful, they are successful.

What great ideas and value are you leaving on the table simply because you aren't asking? It doesn't have to take months and years to set up these innovation channels, just a little bit of forethought and some select process steps and rules of the road. Are you leaving innovation value on the table because you simply haven't asked for input?

CREATE A MENTAL IMAGE OF ENABLING

What does *enable* look like? Have you ever been to a really large water park—I mean the "really" big ones? Got a good image in your mind? (If not, go online to take a look!) How does this represent the *enable* element?

- Think about all the rides—the inputs, the course, the outputs, the twists, and turns!

- Think about the environment—exciting, risk-taking, adventurous, a little scary, but ultimately safe.

- Think about the fun—kids (and adults) squealing on those rides and recounting their daring, death-defying feats of courage or relaxing on the slower, more pleasant rides.

That is what *enabling* looks like! Lots of moving parts at the park equals lots of innovation channels: All the excitement within all the proper boundaries to make sure that, while there may be some bumps and bruises, nobody is going to get seriously hurt. It's fun to be a part of the action— it's contagious and exciting! It's also a bit scary and an adventure! This is what you can envision when you think of *enabling*.

As you review the following chapters describing five channels of enablement, pay special attention to the underlying principles to implement each channel and both the direct and indirect value you expect to get from implementing these channels. The first channel is an open submission process. The results here are just as much about employee engagement and setting a cultural tone as they are about coming up with breakthrough ideas. This engagement and tone can set the stage for more results and value creation in other innovation channels.

CHAPTER 6

Open Submission

Necessity is the mother of invention.

—Anonymous

Sometimes it is necessary to innovate just to survive. The sheer necessity of "needing to innovate" pushes people extra hard to get the job done. So if innovation is thrust upon you in daily execution, why not put a channel in place to formally capture those ideas as opposed to letting them sit on the sideline so they never see the light of day?

When you are a small company, you tend to do this every day already, though informally. When you have proximity to people, it is easy to huddle and share ideas. But when you have geographic dispersion of staff without easy access to people to vet ideas and debate what I sometimes call "half-baked ideas," it becomes more difficult. Also, if you have more layers in your organization, sometimes front-line workers may feel intimidated when submitting their ideas to top leadership. But they would feel more encouraged if they could submit them anonymously.

This chapter explores methods to give employees a channel to suggest their ideas and be recognized or to do so anonymously.

Open submission is by far the easiest innovation channel. It doesn't take a great deal to implement and can instantly produce results. But it does come with some flaws and pitfalls, so pay attention.

THE ORIGINAL OPEN SUBMISSION SYSTEM: THE SUGGESTION BOX

A simple analogy to this channel is the old "General Manager Suggestion Box." Back in those days, one of the easiest ways to capture employee input in a manufacturing environment (or anywhere) was to have a "Suggestion Box" by the employee entrance. If you had an idea, you simply wrote it on a piece of paper and threw it in the box. There were no special rules, forms, or otherwise. This was your direct line to the "General Manager" or someone else who would consider your idea.

An open submission channel also does something intangible for you with the employees. It raises employee engagement. Many times, employees feel like they aren't being listened to. When you have an open submission process and innovation channel, you send a very clear message to employees:

> *"Your input is requested and valued. Thank you for helping to make our company better."*

Being an innovation leader means encouraging people to submit ideas!

Everyone wants a chance to be heard, and this fulfills a basic need we all have as human beings.

This channel is easy and fast to implement. You could go home tonight, grab a box, put some Post-it notes on top with a pen, and begin your "Open Submission Process" tomorrow. It costs very little and can get you some positive employee engagement because now they feel like they have a chance to be heard by submitting their ideas.

A physical box with notes may be a little too basic for your business, though, and you may want to put a little more effort, process, and structure into it. You can accomplish this by setting up a very simple form via e-mail or even an Access database to capture, collect, and organize the inflow and disposition of ideas.

In the end, this is a channel you want to keep relatively simple. The advantage of this channel is its pure simplicity. Don't overthink it—the KISS acronym (keep it short and simple) applies here.

If you have a competitive culture, I'd suggest making this channel a bit of a competition and posting results in a central location, like a corporate cafeteria or intranet. When you post the ideas submitted and implemented and keep a running tally, you can build some competitive spirit in the ranks.

If employees initially struggle with ideation, give them some tools or techniques to brainstorm ideas. There are plenty of tools and books available that stimulate creative thinking and promote ideation. It isn't rocket science; it's structured and unstructured thinking.

Possible Drawbacks of Open Submission

With anything this simple, there can be some troubles that crop up. Here are some things to watch for:

The Suggestion Box can become a joke. Nobody takes it seriously because they don't care. This channel can be more than just a suggestion box, though. It can be a more modern open submission channel where you can control inputs and quality a bit more. If you aren't getting the results you thought you'd get, maybe you haven't created the environment via the *galvanizing* element and need to take a step back and ensure your employees understand why you are soliciting their ideas and the value that you hope to attain and deliver.

Employees don't see their ideas responded to. If you implement an open submission channel to solicit and capture ideas, the fastest way to kill this channel is to turn that channel into a black hole where ideas get submitted but no one ever hears what gets reviewed, considered, or implemented. If you have no idea what happens to the idea, would you continue to submit more ideas? Consider proper communication inputs and outputs.

Not showing some enthusiasm, especially by the executive team, can be a killer. Encourage people to submit ideas! Cast a large and long leadership shadow by encouraging people and then holding them accountable. When you hear problems and complaints in the business, challenge them to respond with a solution—an innovative solution—rather than simply complaining about the problem.

Tips on Making Open Submission Work

To avoid the pitfalls of the suggestion box, there are a few building blocks to consider if you use it as a channel:

1. Make it a little more elegant than an old tissue or office supplies box. Dress it up a little with some company branding and excitement. If you can, go beyond the box to make it a digital channel and capture ideas via e-mail or other ways. Just keep in mind, if you are in a manufacturing environment, a suggestions box may be the most straightforward way to get ideas from front-line employees. Don't forget: Not everyone uses or has access to a computer in their job.

2. Post a notice, physically or digitally, to make it clear what will happen to the idea that is submitted. For example:

   - "We look at the ideas in this channel on the last day of every month," or every two weeks, or whenever you decide. It is important to have a schedule and be consistent with it.

   - "If we believe the idea will add value to our business—for our customers, our employees, our shareholders—we will work to implement it as expeditiously as possible."

- "If the idea is larger and will take more time to evaluate, we will include it for consideration in an appropriate existing business process where it can be vetted more fully, like our budgeting or capital planning cycles."

- "If you would like to be recognized or potentially participate in the evaluation or implementation of this idea, include your name and contact information. We appreciate your contribution and will let you know if and how you can help!"

3. If you do make this a digital channel with the use of e-mail, create a simple form for people to submit their ideas. It's easy to set up an "Innovation Inbox" in Outlook and have all ideas submitted to it. Then have someone responsible for reviewing and responding to the ideas and communicating disposition decisions.

4. A step beyond an Outlook inbox could be using an Access database. Again, you could build a simple form in Access and set up a link on your intranet site. If you are going to route a little technology in this channel due to size, number of ideas, or because you simply want a little more sophistication, consider the following as some of the things you may want to ask on your form—but don't make it too long, or people won't want to fill it out!

- *Name*—if it is okay to contact them for follow-up, but leave an option of anonymity.

- *Department*—so you can analyze where ideas are or aren't coming from. You can also report on this and create some playful rivalry between departments to be the most innovative.

- *Statement of the idea*—limit the input field so they can't ramble on, but you could also put in a minimum amount of words so you don't get the proverbial three-word suggestion without any real thought behind it.

- *Cost*—any indication they can give about the costs to implement. This may be helpful information in evaluation, but it also sets a tone that cost is definitely a consideration.

- *Value*—similar to cost, submitters should give some thought to value: Why should we do this? There has to be a payoff, and if they haven't thought that through—at least a little—is it really a suggestion or just a complaint?

- *Implementation*—would you like to be involved? If someone has an idea, give them a chance to be part of the implementation. Who would be more passionate than the originator of the idea? It may not always work, and people may not always want to implement their own ideas, but at least ask; it can lead to some high levels of employee satisfaction.

With all of the above, you could set up maximum response sizes and require all fields to be filled out so that you don't get incomplete ideas, which can greatly improve the quality of your submissions and set expectations about submissions. Again, just be sure not to get too restrictive or structured that people don't want to take time to submit their idea.

5. Communicate the number of ideas implemented and give the actual suggestions or some samples. Don't just list the winners, but also those ideas that didn't make it. People can see they should submit ideas whether or not they think they will work and that not everything makes the cut.

6. Ready to move to a more advanced level with this channel? Consider opening it up to customers and suppliers. If your employees have great ideas, imagine what your customers and suppliers may come up with. You can run contests for ideas submitted, give company merchandise to customers or suppliers that enter something, or do a multitude of other things to solicit their input and recognize them. Similar to improving employee satisfaction, giving customers and suppliers a channel to offer suggestions and ideas can drive customer satisfaction and retention and supplier loyalty. (See Chapter 10 on the crowdsourcing channel for more information on this concept.)

MAKE OPEN SUBMISSION AN ONGOING PROCESS

Because this is an easy channel, there isn't a lot to maintain as you go forward. You should give some thought to how to communicate results; over time, you could switch up the open submission idea a bit to submit ideas during town halls or other meetings. One idea is to do themed submissions for "improvements during the holiday season" or some other themed submission just to keep things interesting and lively.

One thing to keep in mind with this channel as an ongoing process is tracking. Be sure you maintain an inventory of ideas submitted, evaluated, implemented, and put on hold for later consideration. Don't lose these ideas and results! Just because a submitted idea wasn't developed at the time doesn't mean that it may not apply in the future. You may want to make it an annual process to go back and mine through past ideas that were put on hold or tabled for one reason or another to see if the idea would now create value in the current business environment.

Eventually, this channel can dry up with ideas and could get exhausting after a few months of submissions. Don't be discouraged by that. Maybe take a break from the open submission for a period of time, then bring it back. Simply find ways to mix it up and keep it fresh.

A key metric of success in this innovation channel is simply *participation*. The sheer number of ideas you get in this channel should tell you if employees are accepting of your desire to innovate and capture their ideas. If you aren't getting ideas, you may not have set the right culture, or you may need to consider incentives. You can and should measure the value created from these ideas as well, but really what you want from this channel is a consistent volume of basic ideas for improvement. You should show your employees that their ideas matter and raise employee engagement.

I recommend using a very simple classification system to categorize ideas as they come in so you can evaluate and manage them. For example, here are a few simple classifications to manage ideas coming through the funnel:

- Excellent—implement
- Evaluate—needs refinement or improvement
- Remote
- No, idea has already been tried or implemented
- No, deemed to be not a good idea or not aligned with our strategy

These last two classifications may feel a bit harsh, and they are judgmental. Keep in mind that this is "innovation governance," not "innovation feel good about anything you ever submit." Sorry. You can't have a false expectation that all ideas will be good. All should be submitted, but it's likely that not all will get implemented. It is inevitable that some ideas can and will be bad ideas for your company. However, you don't have to be condescending or a tyrant in your response—simply say thank you for the idea, but no thanks. Also, tracking ideas that aren't good, that have already been considered, or have already been implemented gives you a couple of data points on your employee population and how engaged and knowledgeable they are about your business—current and future state.

BOTTOM LINE

Every business should try a version of this channel at one point or another. It's easy to put into place, doesn't require much maintenance, and aids employee satisfaction. As an innovation leader, keep some perspective on this channel. It may not give you the next major product line or immediate idea that needs to be patented, but it can give you some legitimate, good ideas to consider in your business, and it may be one of the best ways to better engage your employees on real issues in the business.

And don't take lightly the fact that you are giving employees a channel to be heard.

> *"Emotionally, individuals seek recognition of their value, not as 'labor,' 'personnel,' or 'human resources,' but as human beings who are treated with full respect and dignity and appreciated for their individual worth regardless of hierarchical level. Intellectually, individuals seek recognition that their ideas are sought after and given thoughtful reflection and that others think enough of their intelligence to explain their thinking to them."*[19]

Employees want to be respected as individuals, not as "labor" that is just a means to an end. Having this channel available should be well received by employees.

Now the stakes and the value should begin to rise. The next chapter looks at moving beyond open ideation for employees to instead provide some structure and ask them to solve specific problems. In many ways, it's an easier channel for employees to respond to because it has some rules and parameters within which to innovate. While that may sound restrictive, it actually allows for more clear problem solving and, thus, greater value in your business!

CHAPTER 7

Business Challenges

*Never tell people how to do things. Tell them what to do, and
they will surprise you with their ingenuity.*
— General George Patton

Whereas the open submission channel provided no limitations as to what
employees could submit, this channel should be very prescriptive in
approach. Creating a business challenge channel simply formalizes the
way in which you ask employees or teams of employees to solve business
problems. Yes, employees should be solving problems and business challenges every day, and they do. But many times, some of these problems
cross divisions or departments, have multiple implications, or require multiple people to solve or implement a solution. They can also simply be a
problem that needs to be solved quickly, and you want to ideate solutions
quickly to improve the business.

Don't underestimate the competitive spirit of employees and the fun and
creativity that can be unleashed when you have a contest or challenge
for them to engage. Consider General Patton's quote above: Give people
a problem to solve, and stand back and let them solve it. You may get
spectacular results! I've seen the results of this channel firsthand. It can be
contagious in driving more employees to solve problems!

SUGGESTIONS FOR ESTABLISHING A BUSINESS
CHALLENGE CHANNEL

Setting up a business challenge channel is fairly straightforward. Pose a
business problem to employees. Supply them with parameters and data
associated with the problem. Then stand back and let them ideate!

One key in this channel is to pick the right level of problem to solve. It
should be a meaty issue with challenges that will engage employees to formulate ideas of their own. But it should not be so difficult a problem that
nobody has ever been able to solve it. Don't set employees up for failure.
Find a middle ground in problem complexity, and vary that complexity
over time to find your company's sweet spot in offering solutions to these
challenges.

Here are some questions you might ask:

- What creative suggestions can I make about new product ideas?
- How can I cut costs and increase production?
- What new product is needed? What extension of a current product's market?
- How can we sell 20% more than the present?
- How can we better handle customer complaints?
- How can we become more customer-oriented?
- Where are our bottlenecks?
- What could we organize better?
- In what ways could we make more money for our business?[20]

Be careful that you set the right tone in the challenge up front. Don't be judgmental of the functional area that is the source of the issue being solved. That is, if you are solving an issue in the operations area, be sure to point to the *business* issue, not use the challenge to point out a *personnel* issue or department failure or shortcoming. Nobody in a functional area wants to be called out in front of his or her peers.

Also consider the indirect messages you're sending to all employees—the big picture—by highlighting the business problem. You're telling them what is important enough to the executive team to solicit employee input and feedback. They are asking the entire employee population for input. And while only a fraction of employees may respond, everyone hears and sees the message being sent.

It has been my experience in business that more people are inherently good problem solvers, and fewer people are naturally creative ideators. That is, if you give people a specific problem and ask them to solve it, they can come up with solutions based on their experience—both professional and personal. In contrast, if you simply ask people for ideas, where do they start? They're likely to think, *What kind of idea do you want? I'm not creative, I don't invent things!* We aren't all wired to be creative thinkers and come up with the next iPhone, but many of us solve problems all day long. Therefore, give employees a problem, some basic information and supporting data, and let them suggest solutions.

Many people also *like* to solve problems—if they understand the rules or parameters they must play within. Think of the draw and intrigue of Sudoku and crossword puzzles, not to mention the plethora of trivia games you play at home or in bars testing your knowledge. Don't underestimate people! An engaged workforce that wants to see a business succeed can be a powerful force in providing innovative solutions to business challenge topics. Be clear about the rules of engagement, and don't be afraid to challenge employees.

PITFALLS TO AVOID

Yes, there are some traps in this channel:

- Consider how often you want to go to the employee population with business challenges. Do you create one per month? One per quarter? One per week? (I recommend one per month or every other month to begin with.)

- Consider how many times you can ask for suggestions, how long it takes to vet the responses, and how long it will take to implement solutions. If you aren't careful, this channel can turn into a monster of work. On the other hand, if you're getting great results—fabulous! Throw some more resources at it and keep going! In many circumstances, you will want to start a little slower and not burn out people with too many business challenges.

- Lastly, consider the business issues that you share with employees. If you're asking employees for their suggestions, you should assume that they may be talking about this business challenge at home, at industry events, at cocktail parties, and so on—especially if they submitted the winning idea that gets implemented. So while you want to assume that your employees have good intentions and aren't sharing confidential information, you do need to be considerate of the issue. Decide if it's a problem you want others (especially externally) to know about or if it isn't explicitly confidential.

OTHER FACTORS TO CONSIDER

There are several factors to consider when setting up a business challenge channel. Take a look at these factors and then decide the best implementation for your company to achieve success with this channel.

Who Will Create the Business Challenges?

What is the problem you are going to solve, who is going to review the responses, and who is going to follow through with the implementation of the idea?

> *Ultimate solutions may be a combination of different ideas—I call this leapfrog thinking.*

Instead of asking one individual, it's probably best to have a team that comes up with the business challenges on an ongoing basis. Usually the executive leadership team can do this. Since this group is responsible for leadership, management, business success, and aligning resources to achieve value, it should be uniquely qualified and capable of driving this channel. When you have leadership team meetings, make this channel an agenda item: "What business challenge should we ask our employees to solve this month/quarter?" If you aren't on the executive team yourself but are responsible for implementation and oversight of this channel, you may want to offer the executive team some ideas on problems that could be used in business challenges.

Coming up with business challenges likely won't be a problem for the executive team. Picking the correct one will be slightly harder. Also, at the time you pick the problem, select the executive who will be responsible for reviewing solutions and picking a winner. Ensure you aren't always picking the same executive and functional area for the challenges. No executive wants to see his or her area "picked on" for soliciting help on a continuous basis with numerous business challenges.

How Will You Communicate the Challenge to Employees?

Issue the challenge, ideally via an e-mail blast and a posting for those not on e-mail/computers. State the challenge simply and provide the relevant necessary information, including cost impacts or value lost, where and how people can submit their ideas, and a deadline.

How Much Time Will Employees Have to Submit Ideas?

Give employees about one to two weeks to solve the challenge and submit an idea. If it's anything shorter, they may not have time, or they may even drop the ball on an important deliverable they have in their normal workload, which you certainly don't want to happen.

If you give them any longer, they will lose interest and not deem the challenge to have priority or be important. Give them a deadline and at least one reminder of the deadline.

How Will You Communicate Progress?

Communicate the number of responses you're getting along the way. If you get a lot of responses, great! You have hit something that struck a nerve, and people have solutions.

On the other hand, if you get few ideas, tell people that, too. Make it a double challenge by saying, "We have only received two ideas to date. We know this is a tough challenge, so how would you like to be the one to solve it above all others?" Communicate and motivate them to provide solutions.

How Will You Acknowledge Responses and Follow Up?

When the responses are in, communicate to all submitters that you received their ideas, thank them for their submission, and tell them you may follow up with them if you have questions.

How Will You Review the Ideas?

Review the suggested solutions with the executive in charge of picking the winning solution. You may need to call on the submitter to provide additional thought or details about his or her idea. Don't be afraid to do this, and be supportive of the submitter. The submitter may be apprehensive to do this, but he or she may also be very excited to be called upon to provide additional information. Many employees don't get one-on-one face time with a senior executive in their company. They may be quite excited to have that opportunity (keep this in mind when you give feedback. It's 10 minutes in your schedule, and something they may have waited weeks to have the opportunity to do).

What Will You Do with Multiple Solutions?

Sometimes the winning solution is actually multiple solutions. That is, when you go through all the ideas, the solution may actually be a combination of a couple of solutions. I like to call this "leapfrog thinking." If there is no standout solution among the submissions, many times the best solution can come from a combination of multiple submissions or from taking one submission and developing it even further.

Usually, the executives in charge can be very effective at this if the challenge is in their functional area, and they may have more experience in how to implement the solution by making some tweaks. If you combine several ideas, simply give everyone credit! Don't assume the ideas are sacrosanct and that you can't modify them at all.

MAKE THE BUSINESS CHALLENGE CHANNEL AN ONGOING PROCESS

As you consider ongoing business challenges, consider mixing up the business challenges a bit. Maybe the first business challenge is a problem in operations, and you're asking individuals to submit suggestions to solve the problem. Great! Then make the next one a team challenge. Articulate the business problem to be solved, and ask for people to get two, three, or four fellow employees together to solve the problem as a team. They could get people from around the company, or you could make it a "departmental challenge" to see if Sales can beat Marketing or Accounting can beat IT, and so on.

> **Business challenges can deliver real results to real business issues!**

Team challenges create good camaraderie and spirited competition. If the business challenge is a cross-departmental issue, they will likely need to talk with others to solve the problem anyway, so a team challenge is natural.

There are other ways of keeping the challenges fresh, such as offering different incentives. As a native Minnesotan, I can tell you one of the biggest employee perks during the winter time is a parking spot to get out of the snow! Give some creative awards like that coveted, out-of-the-snow parking spot for the month of January to recognize and reward people who submit winning ideas. That can also serve as a reminder to others of the value provided.

MEASURING THIS CHANNEL IS ABOUT ENGAGEMENT AND RESULTS

When you set up the challenges, you should articulate the business issue and the cost impact or value creation that you want to get from solving the problem. When implementing solutions, it may only get you partial value or cost reduction, but there is still value that accrues and can be tracked.

If you did one challenge a quarter or every other month, think of the results you may be able to get! Consider tracking cumulative channel results as well as the individual results of business challenges. Imagine if your customers, suppliers, and other stakeholders walked into your company lobby and see a chart showing the value impact by all employees over a 12-month window.

If I walked into a company lobby and saw something like that showing good results, I would be impressed that the company is embracing innovation and getting all of its employees to actively contribute. This is the type of activity that leads to an award like "Top Companies to Work At," and you could see that award plaque in the lobby because employees are happy to be able to innovate and have their voices heard.

While you're ultimately striving for results to problems in this channel, overall participation is again a key measurement of success. If you get multiple ideas submitted, it shows that your employees are engaged in trying to better the business. If you aren't getting responses, you either have an engagement issue or a process issue in how you are setting up the channel. If it's an engagement issue, take a trip back to the *galvanizing* element of your innovation elixir.

THE BOTTOM LINE

Remember, most people are natural problem solvers. They do it to survive in their lives every day, and some even actually solve problems for fun. Give employees a problem, and they will find a way to solve it. You have to give them a chance to do so. This channel can create value, camaraderie, and maybe even some third-party validation that your business is a top company to work at!

Open submissions and business challenges are two innovation channels about inclusion. Include as many employees as possible to get ideas, create engagement, and, ultimately, value. The next channel, future sensing groups, is very different. It deals with only a handful of people but creates value in a highly leveraged fashion. And while it may not create as much buzz as the first two channels, the value can be the greatest we've talked about yet!

CHAPTER 8

Future Sensing Groups

Every act of creation is, first of all, an act of destruction.
—Pablo Picasso

You have to be willing to challenge the status quo. Don't be so egotistical that you think things can't be improved and should always stay the way they are. When I talk about innovation around existing processes and think people may get defensive of change, I like to use this phrase: "Honor the past, improve the current, and innovate the future." We can innovate and change things in our businesses, but buy-in is harder if you don't honor what people have done in the past by being "respective destructors and constructors" within our businesses.

As with many initiatives in our businesses, the actual project, idea, or initiative itself isn't always the biggest challenge when solving and implementing; instead, it's the emotions and change management aspects that are involved in the actual change in the business. As you challenge the status quo in your business, a future sensing group (FSG) can be tremendously helpful. In creating an FSG, you create a diverse group of individuals who give you not only the employee pulse on the business but also have a high EQ (emotional intelligence) factor to see beyond projects and ideas and think about emotional and cultural impacts that may be associated with change. This group may turn into your critical thinking group that you can talk to about an idea or project before you take it to the masses.

BENEFITS OF USING FUTURE SENSING GROUPS

An FSG can look at current problems, anticipate or speculate about future problems, ideate solutions, and be a place to test ideas and solutions. If set up and chartered appropriately, this group can be a significant source of intelligence that can give you the general pulse of the employee population, especially in larger organizations where you simply can't interact with the entire workforce.

I've used this innovation channel to generate and test ideas as well as to filter and evaluate information. Earlier versions of this channel included groups that were more like think tanks, heavy on IQ. But as I developed this innovation channel further, these teams became more holistic and had strong emotional intelligence. You need to consider what you want most out of this group and source it appropriately.

> **Use this group to test strategies and quickly identify which ones to implement.**

In creating some of these groups in the past, I've called them by a few different names—The Think Tank, Innovation Roundtable, and Office of Innovation—before arriving at the FSG. I've settled on this last name to be the most descriptive and accepted; believe it or not, the name is important. The name is important to those in the group and who aspire to be part of the group, and it also speaks to your expectations of the group. I wouldn't suggest spending a great deal of time about what to name this group, but give it enough thought so that you achieve the goals you're looking for. The name of this group should convey the charter that these participants have been given, and it should also create an aspiration and reflect an achievement level when individuals are asked to participate in this group.

Another name for the people in an FSG is "kingpins":

> *"Key influencers in the organization who are natural leaders, who are well respected and persuasive, or who have an ability to unlock or block access to key resources. As with kingpins in bowling, when you hit them straight on, all the other pins come toppling down."*[21]

Find the kingpins in your business, put them into this group, create this innovation channel, and watch results be generated in weeks, not months or years. In many cases, if you drew a power and influence diagram of your company showing who in the organization has power and influence, many of the folks who fall into the category of largely influential but likely also have some level of middle management "power" should end up in the FSG.

If you choose to create this innovation channel, there are multiple benifits if you do it right:

1. *This group can work together to solve business problems as a team* that requires deeper conversation and review. This team-based approach goes beyond a team business challenge and creates a group of people that can work together continuously and solve issues. This will only get faster with tenure and experience together.

2. *This group can work as a representative group for all employees.* If you pick the right people, you should be able to get more frequent

intelligence on how employees are doing, what they are worried about, their satisfaction levels, and what you can be doing as leadership to create more and better alignment of your workforce.

3. *If you solicit the right people for your group*, charter them appropriately and give them executive oversight and access. You should get great results in an accelerated fashion because the group exists and can be readily tapped for input and information.

4. *When you pick the participants on this team, consider the following*:

   • *The team should be cross-functional*. If you have a large company with a large number of departments, you may not be able to have every single area represented, but be as inclusive as possible.

   • *Tap the best people*. Yes, they are already busy—but you know the saying "If you want something done, give it to a busy person because they will always find a way." If you don't put your very best thinkers and facilitators in this group, what message does that send to those individuals and other employees? It should be an honor to be in this group, and a little healthy jealousy from those who aren't asked to participate is just fine.

5. *Consider the value of encouraging this group to develop "leapfrog thinking."* Leapfrog thinking can happen in a group setting where someone comes up with an idea and others build it out further with their own contributions. This can create tremendous synergy and be incredibly intoxicating to the individuals. Have you ever worked with an individual, a mentor, a leader, or peer that you just really gelled with? Ideas come together quickly and have a fast fluidity like you have with few others—you easily and readily build on each other's thinking. It's very stimulating and creates high value in the business.

6. *This group can be an excellent filter and feeder of information* to the executive leadership team for planning and execution. When leading strategy or innovation efforts, you sometimes come up with ideas but don't know how employees or the executive team will respond. In those cases, use the FSG as your test group: Pitch the idea to the FSG first and get critical input and feedback.

The same goes for monitoring marketing turbulence in your business. As you go through this periodic process, let the FSG be the first group to review the inputs and assess the turbulence when you get the raw information and data. When you take that information to the executive leadership team, you'll have the raw intelligence as well as some thoughtful analysis (presumably from some of your top thinkers in the business) and some pre-filtering of what is important and what is irrelevant.

7. ***This group can also serve as a great way to get a pulse of your best and brightest leaders***. When going through other change initiatives, and maybe even wearisome events like a merger or acquisition, it is nice to be able to quickly get the pulse of the key leaders and managers to see where they stand.

PITFALLS TO AVOID

This channel should be fairly easy to grasp and conceive how you could use it, but the following are some warnings to consider when forming the FSG and using it in an ongoing fashion:

1. ***Beware of picking the wrong people to participate***. Regardless of what you call the group or how you charter it, this channel fails quickly if you pick the wrong people. Red flags to look for: people who don't work well with others, people who are very egotistical and "have all the right answers," people who can't listen but only wait to talk, people who don't commit (showing up late or not showing up at all), and people who are not trusted—up or down in the organization.

2. ***Develop a clear charter for the FSG***. If you pull a great group of individuals together who simply sit around the table and stare at each other, that group isn't going to last very long—especially with type-A, hard-charging individuals who won't have time for it. Set some boundaries on what they are expected to accomplish. Give them the support they need, then take a half-step back and let them work.

3. ***Make sure you give the FSG executive access and oversight***. You need to have at least one person from the executive team to sponsor, lead, facilitate, and direct this group. That executive can look at this assignment in two ways: It can either be one more thing to do on an already full plate, or it can be a chance to mentor and guide this group to achieve some great results for the business. I want the leader who looks at this group as an opportunity, not another chore. If you have picked some of the best people in the business, what executive leaders worth their salt would not want to mentor and lead this group? Pick a strong, facilitative leader who cares about the business and about employee development.

4. *Don't let a lack of commitment undermine the FSG*. Schedules change, the business has demands, and customers need to be taken care of. Have some flexibility and avoid anything as draconian as a 100% attendance policy for this group. At the same time, however, you can't let an individual get away with "I'll attend when it's convenient or valuable to my department only." Kick those people off the team and send a message. You know your company and cultural norms best; set up the FSG to succeed in your environment and then ensure the executive sponsor supports it. If participants don't commit to the group, you don't want them.

HOW TO SET UP AN FSG

Next let's talk about building the group and the sequential steps of creating this innovation channel. We know the pros and cons of what can go right and wrong, so keep them in mind as you go through these steps.

> *FSG members are both close to execution and get visibility to market data—let them turn both of these data sources into valuable information.*

1. *Determine an executive sponsor of the group.* This is likely to be the person responsible for strategy and/or innovation for your business. Not only should they have the best preview of issues, challenges, and probability for a solution, but they also would benefit by getting closer to the business via this group of people.

2. *Charter the group*. List what you want the group members to accomplish, the expected norms of the group, and the value that group members will get from participating. Below are only a few examples to consider:

   • The FSG will meet monthly for two hours.

   • The agenda and discussion topics will be provided in advance for reading and review before the meeting.

   • The FSG will be both forward and backward looking.

   • It will analyze past results and current practices to identify improvement areas and lessons learned.

   • It will look at future endeavors by periodically monitoring market and competitor turbulence.

- It will provide input and review of business strategies, initiatives, innovation projects, and other areas deemed significant by the executive sponsor and executive leadership team.

- The FSG will balance timely review and responses with accuracy and sufficient data inputs.

- And so on.

3. *Select the group members.* I typically suggest asking my peers on the executive team or the CEO to "give me one or two nominees from each function that you see as a thought leader, innovator, can-do resource who is energetic and deserving to sit with similar peers to ideate and test ideas in our business based on multiple information sources." You may even have an actual or mental list of these individuals already. They may be identified in HR practices as "Hi-Pos" (high potential talent) or identified in formal or informal departmental succession plans.

From a development standpoint, the list of nominees can be lengthy. Who wouldn't want to be associated with a think tank group and have that recognition from their executives? It can be pretty easy to identify the right folks, but a little harder to pry them loose for participation. The best candidates will want to join and make time for this. They will want the opportunity and executive exposure and know that it will benefit them in the long term.

4. *Have the executive sponsor recruit or talk individually with each participant nominated for the FSG.* Let the sponsor decide who is in the group after talking with individuals from the nomination list and assessing team chemistry.

5. *Finalize the group and launch!*

- Review the skeleton charter, get input from the FSG members, and finalize it.

- Establish an agenda and rhythm for meetings and get everyone to commit to it.

- Identify the first three meetings and what the areas of review, study, and impact will be. This will generate enthusiasm and show the type of value creation that is expected.

6. *Execute, Communicate, and Repeat!*

MAKE SURE THE FUTURE SENSING GROUP'S WORK IS AN ONGOING PROCESS

In business today, the old adage of "information is power" applies to a much smaller extent. Information is rampant and overwhelming today. The power and value is now in *interpretation* and what to do with that information, if anything. Therefore, the idea of an FSG is to determine what to do with the information available and how to turn that information into actionable value to the business, such as using it to predict market trends and, if you are lucky, help shape them.

The FSG needs to look at both risks and opportunities in the business to find good bets that drive more value for the business and clients while taking reasonable risks. This balance can be achieved with a group of smart individuals who are willing to research, test, filter, and execute ideas.

From an ongoing standpoint, you'll need to consider the consistency of the group. Consider a "term limit" or "rotation" of individuals in the group. Stagger changes to ensure consistency and continuity of the group going forward. Some change will naturally occur as individuals switch positions or even leave the company, and business changes can occur that require a change in the group's composition. Plan for this ongoing flux and embrace it.

HOW TO MEASURE THE SUCCESS OF YOUR FSG

There are a few metrics of success with the FSG channel that you can monitor and aspire to, such as:

1. Number and value of specific initiatives designed or implemented by the FSG.

2. Value-added internal consulting reviews or reports. If the FSG monitors market turbulence, offers input on specific business issues, or provides employee engagement insights, all of these culminate in a "consulting report" of some sort. Formalize these, and measure them.

3. FSG team churn and appointments. If people are frequently coming and going from the team, that normally isn't good. If people are waiting and aspiring to get nominated to this team, that is good.

4. Executive Team Efficiency. This may be hard to measure. Consider your strategic planning process or other areas where you may normally iterate multiple times to get results. If an FSG is used successfully upfront, it can drastically improve the efficiency and time

the executive team spends on these activities and actually produces better results.

GETTING STARTED

You may be surprised at the talent that is just waiting to be ignited when you try this innovation channel in your organization! You'll also realize great synergies in pulling together talented individuals to operate as a team. They will challenge and grow from each other. When an FSG is set up appropriately, it can be a great accelerator in your business. Not only will it be a help in designing and implementing innovative solutions, but it will also help in monitoring and assessing issues in your business landscape and competitive environments.

If you believe this channel can be a positive, impactful feeder of information and value to the executive team, try the following as a first assignment. Have them read a business or leadership book—it can be either a classic or maybe something more recent and controversial. I've seen some large corporations routinely do this via a "book club" concept where individuals get together, talk about the theories, concepts, and methodologies within the book, and then debate how the company could benefit from implementing those concepts or why they shouldn't be implemented. This can lead to some very robust discussion on how a business should or could modify its strategies based on new or classic methods. If the group agrees that something is a good idea, then comes the debate on how to take actions to implement these new ideas or processes and who needs to be involved. This may sound like an academic exercise, but consider all the good advice and models that exist—don't you think there is something that can be learned from that?

Don't underestimate the potential value in the FSG channel. It can directly create value for your business, and there's value in having a filter of information and analysis to feed to the executive team as well as the value of mentoring and further developing some of your top talent in the organization.

An FSG is a team-based channel. Next, Chapter 9 will go in the other direction and focus on the most exclusive channel, fellowships. You might have only one person participate directly in this channel in a year, but the payoffs and results can be monumental.

CHAPTER 9

Fellowships

A life spent making mistakes is not only more honorable, but more useful than a life spent doing nothing.
—George Bernard Shaw

Have you ever been in a job where you had a great idea for a new product, service offering, or some other a significant way to create value but simply didn't have the time, resources, or access to decision makers to have your idea heard? This situation can be frustrating for anyone. Sometimes employees get put in the wrong seats on the bus and could run circles around their managers. Other times, they simply have an idea but no channel to get support for it. It might even get to the point where the individual ends up leaving your company over the frustration of not being heard or given the opportunity to shine.

Creating a fellowship innovation channel can solve this issue and create tremendous value to your organization. Fellowships are meant to get at creative, innovative people in the business who have those "big ideas" but no avenue to bring them forth.

And for the individuals who consider submitting a fellowship proposal but are nervous, heed George Bernard Shaw's advice—Go for it, or you'll have regrets!

ANNOUNCING YOUR FELLOWSHIP PROGRAM

Imagine being at your company and seeing the e-mail or posting shown in Exhibit 9-1.

Exhibit 9-1: Sample E-mail/Sign Promoting Fellowships to Encourage Innovation from Employees

ALL EMPLOYEES:

Do you have a big idea for our business?

Do you have an entrepreneurial itch but need a safe environment and resources?

Do you need some time to explore and run with this idea?

> *Today is your lucky day! You may be eligible to be selected to work on a project that you deem to have great interest and value in our business for the next six months, either full- or part-time. Your current job responsibilities would be covered by a colleague (pending supervisor approval), and you'll return to your job after your fellowship is complete—unless you are greatly successful and create a new position for yourself based on the fellowship work!*
>
> *You will be assigned an executive coach as a mentor to help you navigate the organization to get the resources you need. Your mentor will serve as a sounding board as you work through execution, help to motivate you, and keep you on track. Today may be the day you get to bring your idea to life and implement it in our business!*
>
> *We will be accepting Fellowship applications through the end of the month. Let us know your big idea to create value for our business or customers!*
>
> *Good Luck!*

For a hungry, talented type-A person, this sounds like a dream! Getting to be an internal entrepreneur. Getting to scratch that itch in a low-risk environment. I think this is a smart program and approach to get big ideas on the table, create some excitement in the organization, drive employee morale, and ultimately innovate to drive business results. If you do this right, you will create intense competition among projects and generate high employee satisfaction—what CEO or innovation leader doesn't want that kind of environment?

One example is a business that has a program where researchers can use 15% of their time to investigate whatever they like, and proven researchers or innovators get up to 50%. Fifty percent!! Now *that* is unleashing your resources to drive for results! Although you may not be able to allow this much time and focus on innovation ideation and experimentation in your business, a fellowship program may be a step in the right direction.

> **This program can evaluate and groom future leaders in a live environment.**

HOW THE FELLOWSHIP PROGRAM WORKS

A fellowship innovation channel could almost be described as a sabbatical, except it is a sabbatical that is a competition and grants resources to a worthy business idea. Stuck under the thumb of your manager? Here is your shot at fame and fortune! If you have an idea for a new product, service, offering, or something in your business that would drive significant value, then this is the innovation channel for you. In this channel, you would submit your idea to a fellowship committee. The committee would review the idea. If they award you the fellowship, here is what it could look like:

- You are freed up from your current position for at least 75% of your time to work on this project.

- You will lead the project and have access to an executive mentor (someone on the executive team) who can help you navigate business hurdles, make decisions, and keep the project moving along when you encounter sticking points. You will be given access to resources—people, funding, and so on—needed for the project.

- You will review progress and end results with your mentor and the innovation committee that sponsored your fellowship.

- If you have created a new product, service, or offering that requires ongoing support, you may be asked to lead or support this new offering in a variety of capacities.

This is an individual's shot at the brass ring, but in a safe environment without betting their personal resources—but they are using the company's resources so they will be held accountable. What is the value to the company? It's a shot at the next distinctive or breakthrough product, service, or process for its business. And as with many companies, culture is everything! Creating this channel should send a cultural message—innovation is important, sought, and valued! This channel allows people to implement something that's significant in their company and that they have a profound interest in.

BENEFITS OF IMPLEMENTING A FELLOWSHIP PROGRAM

There are several benefits to implementing a fellowship channel. Consider the following:

1. *Increased employee satisfaction*—although you may award only one or two fellowships in a given year, EVERY employee has a shot at it and can only fault themselves for not trying. You may send the winner of the fellowship over the moon with excitement, but you are implementing a channel in which anyone can have a shot to realize a dream, make a difference, be recognized, be a leader in the business, learn a tremendous amount, and advance his or her personal career. How many companies have you been in

where all employees were at least given the opportunity to take a shot like this?

2. ***Grooming future leaders*** — a program like this is perfect to evaluate and groom future leaders in your business. You are giving someone access to resources and mentorship. In turn, you get to evaluate and watch that person's success or failure and how he or she handles it all. Even if the fellowship fails to achieve its goals, you still could have an "A" player with a "C" idea, and I'll take that over a "C" player with an "A" idea any day because you have the chance to mentor and develop that "A" player into something more.

3. ***Mentee/Mentor opportunities*** — sometimes we can put mentor/ mentee programs in place that are well intended but don't really produce results. They are more of a feel-good program. This channel — having a solid mentee paired with a thoughtful mentor — can create an efficient working environment that yields significant business results. It's a live learning and teaching lab, and there is no better teacher than experience itself!

4. ***Rabid Commitment*** — in seeing a few of these fellowships and the people who get the opportunity, this is one thing I look forward to and see 99% of the time: rabid commitment. The individuals who apply for this fellowship opportunity are driven. If given the chance to succeed, they will move heaven and earth to get the job done. I can only think of those words "rabid commitment" to describe their ferocious pursuit of their goal. Don't you wish you had this level of enthusiasm in all your projects?

PITFALLS TO AVOID

On the flip side, there are some traps to look out for when introducing and executing this program. Consider the following:

1. ***If you are going to implement a fellowship program, commit to it***. Don't just say the words and anoint some poor fool to work on a project after hours or off the side of their plate on top of their existing job. Give them the time to work on the project seriously and the resources to support them. Otherwise, good luck getting real ideas and candidates.

2. ***Provide a real mentor***. What do I mean by a real mentor? A few things:

   - They are leaders in the organization and can get things done. That is, they are respected and can remove hurdles for the fellowship participant.

- They have high EQ to go with their high IQ. That is, they understand relationships and have excellent soft skills, which they will exhibit and teach their mentee, showcasing the importance of influence vs. power in achieving business goals.

- They commit to mentoring the individual. They don't reschedule a review three times due to other priorities. Yes, schedules inevitably change, but they have to make this project a priority and lead their influential mentee by example. At the same time, they can't take over the project and deprive the individual of the learning experience. Similar to what we say to board members at companies, mentors need to "keep your noses in, but your fingers out" of the project.

3. *Give solid consideration to the number of fellowships you'll award in a given year*. If one is good, 10 is better, right? *Not necessarily.* Be thoughtful of the number of resources and time commitment a fellowship can take. If you try to do too many too fast, you may get subpar results. Also, doing too many fellowships may undermine other business processes. This fellowship program needs to work *in conjunction* with other processes, not *in competition* with them. It shouldn't overtake other standard business processes you have in place.

4. *Have a balanced risk view in assessing fellowships and selecting winners*. You want individuals to take risks and learn from what they do, but you don't want them to fail entirely, thereby not returning business value or leading others to label the fellowship program a bust. This is a challenge that needs to be managed thoughtfully.

HOW TO ESTABLISH A FELLOWSHIP PROGRAM

I've outlined a number of the dos and don'ts in implementing this program, but let's specifically look at the actions that need to be taken to get this channel off the ground:

1. *Discuss this channel with the executive leadership team* and get their buy-in to support, promote, and sponsor the program by providing resources and mentors.

2. *Outline the program—* document and describe the program so that others will understand it. Capture the goal of the channel as a whole and what the company expects to get from the program.

> *Be thoughtful about the number of fellowships you award—make sure the organization is ready.*

3. *Share the program with the entire employee population and be excited!* Make it a big splash. Have your CEO and others on the leadership team voice their support and excitement in wanting to see the fellowship ideas that are submitted.

4. *Clarify the resources that will be available* and rules of engagement around employees getting time off their regular position if they're awarded the fellowship.

5. *Create an application form for people to submit their fellowship ideas.*

6. *Capture, evaluate, and respond to the fellowship applications* and follow up with specific individuals on fellowship ideas as needed.

7. *Interview those with the top 3–5 fellowship ideas.* Have them pitch their idea to you, the evaluator, or to a committee that will chose the winner. I highly recommend having a small committee of two or three leaders from the executive team listen to the pitches and select a winner. This does a couple of things. First, it gets those executives to buy into the program by participating in the evaluation process and offering counsel. Second, the fellowship applicants get a fuller executive audience and better understand the gravity of their submission and that their idea is being taken seriously.

8. *Select the idea that will be awarded* and, depending on what the idea is and what functional area it impacts, select an appropriate mentor.

9. *Talk with the contributor's immediate manager* to discuss and arrange backfill in the position and to work through how the manager can support the applicant moving into the fellowship role.

10. *Make the announcement and award the fellowship!* Congratulate the individual and share the next steps. Include his or her supervisor in that conversation. Also make the introduction to the mentor and encourage that person to immediately set up a rhythm of meetings to launch, execute, and monitor the fellowship project.

11. *Provide periodic updates and communications* about the progress being made in the fellowship to the executive team and all employees as appropriate. Don't let this be a secret project; instead, let others see what is going on. As they watch the fellowship develop, you may be recruiting the next set of people who will submit fellowship applications.

12. *Close the project or transition it to normal operations as appropriate*. Conduct a post-mortem from a mentor and mentee standpoint and officially close and report on the project.

MAKE FELLOWSHIPS AN ONGOING PROCESS

As you consider the ongoing nature of this program, don't wait for the first one to be complete before you begin planning for the next application process. After you have determined the number of fellowships you want to do in a year, I suggest beginning to plan and schedule for the second one when the first is about 75% complete.

Think about lessons learned from the first cycle and apply them to the second fellowship cycle. If there are many lessons learned and surprises, wait for the post-mortem before you start another round. If the results are fairly predictable and the program has been successful, get a new round of enthusiasm going and work to launch a second fellowship even while the first is in the final stages.

HOW TO MEASURE THE SUCCESS OF A FELLOWSHIP PROGRAM

Measurements around this innovation channel come in two forms:

1. *The number and quality of fellowship submissions*. If the pipeline is weak, it will likely be a weak program. If the program is robust with a lot of good ideas to choose from, results should be robust.

2. *Actual results from each fellowship*. This should be straightforward to track and communicate since the intended results of each fellowship idea should be clearly delineated in the proposal and tracked if implemented.

Give someone the opportunity to run with their big idea in your company. In addition to the potential business value, employee morale should take a nice tick up as employees see you empowering them to do their best!

Be thoughtful in the number of projects you award and what you do with other good ideas that are relevant and worthy of review but aren't a full fellowship. Think of this channel as unleashing people in your business to get their big ideas out there, tested, and, in some cases, implemented. This could turn into an incubation channel to launch new product lines and businesses within your business. If successful, you may find yourself trying to figure out how to award numerous innovation fellowships due to the quality of ideas and potential value creation—what a great problem to have!

So far, the innovation channels have been internally focused. The last innovation channel looks at sources outside the company. Best practice research says we should get about 50% of our ideas from outside our own company! Who should you crowdsource with? What topics should you address? With what goals? Let's press on to find out.

CHAPTER 10

Crowdsourcing

No idea is so outlandish that it should not be considered.
—Winston Churchill

You've heard the saying "There is no such thing as a dumb question," right? Well, with innovation, Winston Churchill's quote is right, too, and I think a little more on point. Any idea could be a good idea, or at least it should be considered further before being dismissed. Ideas may need to be fleshed out. They may have been tried before but failed. The timing could have been wrong for them, or maybe they are simply wrong. *But* don't stifle ideas by judging them immediately. They may be good ideas and worthy of additional consideration and debate. Ask clarifying questions and peel back the onion a few layers to see what is beneath. Give ideas a chance!

Along that line, ideas can also come from any source—not just from within the company. When you are innovating, share the fun and challenge! Ask your suppliers. They want to be partners and strategic, so give them the chance to be so. Ask your clients/customers. Henry Ford was quoted as saying, "*If I'd asked people what they wanted, they would have asked for a better horse.*" And it's true, sometimes customers don't know what they want. But many times they do know (and don't forget—they are the ones who write the check for your products/services).

Challenge anyone who will listen—entrepreneurs with open headspace, think tanks, universities, industry associations, and so on. Get ideas from a multitude of places for diversity of ideas and inclusion of different opinions and ideas. Sometimes organizations get very inwardly focused when they are solving problems and looking at innovation, forgetting to give their customers the chance to offer input.

The big picture on this innovation channel is simple. Get innovation support, input, and ideas from anywhere and everywhere. The adage of "if one head is good, two are better" applies here. Get many heads engaged. This provides a diversity of thoughts and enables the application of ideas and concepts from areas *outside* of your business and industry. You may find some of the most insightful innovation ideas coming from outside your four walls and even from an industry totally unrelated to your own. (Remember PDEs from Chapter 2!)

Remember how the IMA research showed that a high percentage of companies are not taking advantage of this channel and potentially leaving good ideas on the table without even asking! The pros and cons of a crowdsourcing channel are similar to those for the open submission channel discussed in Chapter 6, but there are enough differences that you don't want to confuse the channels; they are indeed different in how you solicit ideas and provide feedback.

Getting ideas from the outside world helps to keep your thinking fresh. Sometimes companies hire leaders and talent from outside their industry just to come in and shake things up. They want these new leaders to bring new ideas and challenge the status quo, not be "burdened" by past knowledge. The same applies here when implementing this channel.

Also consider how you interact with your stakeholders—specifically, customers and suppliers. Do you regularly provide them a channel to provide input and have their voices heard? What do you think they would say if you told them you valued their input and had a formal channel in which to capture, review, and evaluate their suggestions? I'd bet it would be positive. In today's digital age, you can use crowdsourcing methods for very fast, economical, and repetitive ways to get real market insights and feedback on innovation value creation plans.

PITFALLS TO AVOID

Anytime you begin to open up a program or idea to areas outside of your four walls, you need to be careful. If it's going to the outside world, you could find this information on the cover of a major newspaper or blog, in a bad way, so consider and plan around the following areas:

1. *Carefully choose who you ask about each problem.* Be careful in what you share with various constituents. The business challenge channel asks employees to solve a current business issue. I don't think a "business challenge" idea on how to improve an operational issue may be palatable to the outside world. A business or operational problem that you have might be seen as a weakness that you don't know how to fix yourself. Sometimes suppliers should be brought in to solve these types of problems, but not customers. Generally, you should ask the outside world about how you can provide more and better value across your existing value proposition, which is already known in the marketplace.

> **Be thankful that one of your stakeholders took the time to give you feedback—thank them all!**

2. *Pay attention to social media*. You could use a social media channel to solicit and capture ideas while also monitoring negative posts/ tweets via these channels. Be careful and have deliberate plans for social media.

3. *Be responsive*. Remember the black hole of communications from the open submission channel? That applies here even more so! While you don't want to be unresponsive to your employees and their ideas in an open submission channel, you absolutely DO NOT want to be unresponsive to your customers or critical suppliers! If they submit an idea, you better respond back. At minimum, a simple thank you is needed. Hopefully, you can provide more feedback and, if appropriate, share the input or feedback with your client account management or vendor-relations team as appropriate. Then they can be aware of the suggestions and better manage the entirety of the relationship.

HOW TO SET UP A CROWDSOURCING CHANNEL

There are several steps to take depending on the type of crowdsourcing you are going to do. Let's start with some clarifying questions:

1. Who do you want to reach out to? Suppliers, customers, universities, and so forth.

2. Do you want to reach out to anyone and everyone in these constituent groups, or do you want to segment and only reach out to specific subsets? That is, do you want to limit it to only the top 10 suppliers, suppliers that have been around more than five years, top customers by revenue, top customers by years of relationship, satisfied customers, dissatisfied customers, regional universities, research universities, and so on.

3. What do you want to ask them? If this is an innovation channel, it will probably be something along the following lines:

   • What new feature would you most like to see on our core product?

   • What new product would you like to see us bring to market?

   • What do you see as our greatest strength in what we provide to you?

   • What do you see as an area of improvement in how we serve you?

   • If you could tell our CEO a way in which we could drive more value to you, what would you say?

4. How will you solicit input from these stakeholders?

- Put a simple form on your company website

- Use a crowdsourcing technology to organize distribute and report results

- Hold a workshop at their location

- Simple e-mail responses

- Other

> *Crowdsourcing today can be very fast via social media and very cheap via 3D prototyping—why would you not take advantage of it?!*

After you have addressed most of these questions, you will have better identified your focus of crowdsourcing. Then you can move to these basic process steps:

1. Formulate "the ask"—what do you want them to provide?

2. Identify your solicitation and collection vehicle.

3. Make the ask!

4. Review submissions and thank each person. It can be a custom thank you or something system-generated, depending on the population you are soliciting and the volume of submission. Make sure that other departments like Client Account Management, Sales, or Operations are in the loop on these communications, as they manage these relationships day to day and should be aware of this communication.

5. Give feedback. If you are asking a top supplier, customer, or other stakeholder for input and don't give them any feedback on their idea, you may jeopardize the relationship. Don't do that! Be thoughtful and thankful for the idea. At minimum, tell them you have received their idea and will evaluate it further.

MAKE CROWDSOURCING AN ONGOING PROCESS

If you envision doing this multiple times and with multiple stakeholder sets, I highly recommend getting some technology to facilitate and manage the process. Any specific recommendations on crowdsourcing technology will be dated as soon as I write them in a book, so I won't make any. Simply do some research on some of the best crowdsourcing platforms that are available and evaluate them against what you'd like to get out of them. The 10 questions listed in Exhibit 10-1 should help you evaluate the solutions.

Exhibit 10-1: Questions to Ask about Any Possible Solution

1. Is this software I install on my hardware, or is it a platform as a service, software as a service, or some other type of solution?

2. What is the scalability of the solution? Can I manage multiple "campaigns" or innovation challenges with it?

3. Can I manage multiple constituents (i.e., crowdsource from employees, suppliers, customers, general public, and do them all together or separately as I desire)?

4. Does it have a voting feature that can be turned on internally and/ or externally? (I've seen solutions where individuals can submit ideas and people vote for the ideas they like best. This is great for building consensus and gives you quick market feedback!)

5. Can I build on other's ideas? (Leapfrog thinking! Some software allows you to "post" a reply to an idea to elaborate on it and take it to another level).

6. What is the cost?

7. What is the time to implement?

8. What is the reporting ability?

9. What is the archiving ability?

10. Can I tie this to my e-mail solution so as to manage communications via e-mail?

MEASURING THE RESULTS OF CROWDSOURCING

You can measure the results of this channel in two basic categories: Current Improvements/Enhancements and New/Future Concepts. I don't view either category as better or worse than the other. As a matter of fact, a balance of innovation ideas in both categories is something you would want to see. You want to innovate and improve your current value proposition, and you want to make your products/services better, cheaper, faster, and drive more value to your customers.

You'll also want to get input on future features, products, services, or other value-add components of your value proposition. You want to take the constituent input and research the areas and ideas they involve. The applicable ideas can be fed into your new product development process and potentially your strategic planning process as you look to advance, accelerate, and grow the business and the value the company provides.

BOTTOM LINE

There are a number of constituents that can provide meaningful feedback and input. Not all the input will be gold; just acknowledge and accept what you receive, and dig for the gold nuggets that you do get.

Many of the same internal rules apply to these external constituents—be thankful of the ideas they submit, respond to them, recognize them as appropriate, and let them know they are important and being listened to. Be sure you include other functional areas when you communicate with constituents so that those areas know that their assigned customers, suppliers, and so forth are providing ideas and inputs and that you are communicating with them. Don't let your colleagues be surprised and impact the relationship negatively. This channel should strive to create better, more strategic, and valuable relationships.

ONE MORE CHANNEL: LIGHTS, CAMERA...INNOVATION DAY!

As we get to the end of the discussion on innovation channels, I'd like to suggest one additional "event" that is sort of a combination of several channels: hold an Innovation Day. This type of event requires thoughtful, comprehensive planning and preparation to be successful. If you think an Innovation Day could be successful at your organization, at minimum consider the following:

Innovation Day Goals

- *Create innovation excitement*—Create excitement in the employee population and show leadership's commitment and emphasis to innovation.

- *Showcase what good examples look like*—Create an exposition of some of the best innovations from the past year to inspire other employees, showcase the developments for outsiders, and recognize top innovators.

- *What else do you want to achieve from an Innovation Day?* Include your own goals for an Innovation Day.

Innovation Day Considerations

- Bring in an external speaker who can talk in a town hall environment and motivate, inspire, and review innovation essentials with your entire employee population.

- Distribute a leadership report about innovation value created over the last relevant timeframe—likely the past year—and include a forecast for expectations and targets for the next year.

- Include an "expo" that showcases top innovations from across the company. Have innovators explain their innovations—how they were conceived, designed, and implemented and an update on their current state.

- Open the expo and guest speaker session to outsiders—suppliers, customers, Wall Street analysts, and so on. Share and showcase your innovation success with everyone and solicit and encourage them to participate going forward.

- Hold a recognition ceremony, dinner, or reception for top innovators. Whether you create an "Innovation Hall of Fame" or some other recognition program, do something—anything—to recognize the innovators for their efforts and to inspire others.

- If you have multiple locations, be clear about who can or can't— and should or shouldn't—attend. Be as inclusive as possible while keeping the business operating. There are compensating factors for those who can't make it, such as providing other plants and sites with a live stream from an Innovation Day at corporate headquarters, recording keynote sessions, or filming a video walkthrough of the expo for employees to view remotely or after the event.

An Innovation Day can be a very powerful event, but you have to be thoughtful in planning it and commit to a solid, worthwhile event.

ACTION: Before proceeding to the next chapter, use the following form as a worksheet to reflect on the Enablement chapters—the second element of your Innovation Elixir. What were your key takeaways from these chapters, and how will you customize these tools and principles to drive value in your company? In what order will you sequence these channels so they will work in your organization? Which should you implement first? If you already tried a channel before and failed, how will you do it differently to ensure success this time? Don't wait until the end of the book—begin formulating your Innovation Elixir NOW!

replace with LOGO

GOLD NUGGETS
APPLICATION AT MY BUSINESS

THREE Gold Nuggets you are taking away as foundational elements of your innovation strategy, items for discussion and contemplation at your business with your teams, or concepts that need further research: *(circle one)*

1. *FOUNDATIONAL / DISCUSS / RESEARCH* _____

2. *FOUNDATIONAL / DISCUSS / RESEARCH* _____

3. *FOUNDATIONAL / DISCUSS / RESEARCH* _____

Concept to Execution → which concepts will I implement at our business?

Implement Immediately: **Reserve/Consider Later**

A. _____   C. _____

B. _____   D. _____

Innovation Elixir – The Secret Potion at My Business.

What specific tweaks would I need to make to achieve success at my business, with its unique culture, employees & leadership?

1. _____

2. _____

3. _____

PART IV

The Third Element: Measuring Innovation—It Only Counts If It Adds Value!

Innovation has nothing to do with how many R&D dollars you have. When Apple came up with the Mac, IBM was spending at least 100 times more on R&D. It's not about money. It's about the people you have, how you're led, and how much you get it.

—Steve Jobs

You are on a journey to create an Innovation Elixir, a potion for your business so that you can lead, support, drive, and reap innovation value! This section describes the third element of this potion: measuring. By now, I hope you are discerning the first of the basic ingredients of your core elixir formula. I also hope you have learned about the specific adjustments you'll need to incorporate for success in your business, culture, and environment:

- You have *galvanized* your organization—your employees, suppliers, customers, and other constituents are ready to innovate, and they know that you value, support, and require innovation in your business.

- You have *enabled* your constituents. You have implemented multiple innovation channels—mechanisms that can solicit, collect, evaluate and monitor, and report on innovation projects. You have multiple channels to activate the largest number of your employees, customers, and other constituents because you know that people are different by nature and will respond to different innovation channels. By having multiple channels, you know how to reach as many people for their contributions as possible.

- That now takes us to the last critical element of the Innovation Elixir—the element of *measurement*. Remember the old adage, "If you can't measure it, you can't improve it." This is a key part of innovation governance—you have to be able to measure your results. Why? Because you want to continuously move the bar higher and know that you are indeed creating innovation value, not just innovation activity. Yes, you have to be willing to fail, but have an attitude and mantra of "fail, but fail fast and learn something from it." You also need to measure results and talk about improvement with your employees, customers, and the market.

Remember the buckets of incremental, distinctive, and breakthrough innovations described in Chapter 5? Using those as a basis, you should measure things like these:

> **If you can't measure innovation, how do you know you are generating any value?**

• *Incremental*—operational areas and around customer retention and satisfaction—how can you get improvement and more value *today*?

- *Distinctive*—new programs, new approaches, first movers in the market—how can you drive more value in the *next quarter/year*?

- *Breakthrough*—new business models, acquisitions—how can you shape and lead the industry or outright create new markets *in the future*?

But what are the right metrics, and which ones should you be using to measure innovation value in your business? This is the last area of discussion in this book, and it may be the most important. Being able to measure is like having a compass on a ship. If you can't tell where you are going, how do you know you are heading in the right direction? If you can't measure innovation, how do you know you are generating any value?

CREATE A MENTAL IMAGE OF MEASURING

You know what *galvanizing* and *enabling* look like from the previous chapters—Greek heroes and water parks. So what does *measuring* look like? Clear your mind one last time. Imagine the following images flashing through your mind—like a camera flashing and showing you frame by frame in slow motion:

- A yardstick

- A yin & yang symbol

- A balancing scale

- A smiling customer

- A picture of you rolling the dice in Vegas

- A Sherpa going up the mountain one step at a time

- A baseball game—a single, a double, a triple, and a homer

- A high-wire act, with the performer on a unicycle holding a balancing rod

You should have several images in your mind because painting a picture of the measuring element is not just about one thing, getting to a particular measurement, number, or calculation and then saying "I'm done!" Calculating a metric is only the beginning. It's with that measurement that you can then have dialogue, make more decisions, and get more and better results. The measure element in innovation is iterative and ongoing. Measurement is a constant stride for balance, improvement, and value creation within your innovation governance framework. The picture in your mind should be a series of pictures that tells a story—that is measurement.

As Chapters 11–13 discuss the importance of measuring in your Innovation Elixir potion, keep in mind that you'll have some standards or benchmarks to evaluate against when you measure, but there are also some specific parts about *your* business model and positioning that I can't describe. I can make some generalizations around business strategy archetypes and common benchmarks and apply some experiential principles, but the actions you take in innovation need to be based on *your* business's strategy, capabilities, and vision and *your* overall leadership and guidance. Use these next three chapters to start to have robust discussions around measurement and the actions that you need to take based on what you calculate and predict will happen in your business.

And remember, similar to traditional balanced scorecarding, calculating the measures is not the end point, but rather the beginning. Applying a scorecard framework to measure innovation gives you a measurement *system* with which to measure, monitor, improve, and discuss innovation successes and improvement areas. Measure to drive improvements. Measure to create value for your customers and markets. Measure to win!

The next three chapters share a measurement and management system for innovation. This system will build on some of the principles already discussed, plus a few more. As I wrote this book and tested the system with a pilot group in the IMA research, the following was some of the feedback specific to the overall structure of this model that I'd like you to keep in mind as you go through the measurement chapters and learn about why I believe the Innovation Value Score® (IVS), which I will discuss, is helpful in measuring and managing innovation value.

The survey asked, "In your opinion, do you think the following aspects of the IVS approach would be helpful to your organization?" Here are the results:

	Not helpful	Somewhat helpful	Very helpful	Extremely helpful
Balanced scorecard framework	3%	29%	**52%**	16%
Breakdowns by incremental, distinctive, and breakthrough	3%	**45%**	36%	16%
Breakdowns by leading and lagging indicators	6%	**36%**	32%	26%
Reporting comparisons and actionability	6%	22%	**36%**	**36%**

Using an existing framework like a balanced scorecard can be very helpful in speed of implementation, in adoption, and in overall understanding and communication. Having different cuts (incremental/distinctive/breakthrough innovation and leading and lagging indicators) to compare, contrast, debate, and discuss is helpful in discussions and points to specific focus areas. And more than anything, 72% of respondents like actionability and comparability in reporting! They want to measure these indicators, but they ultimately want to determine steps for improvement in order to drive more value. They also want to review other company's results so they can be more competitive, more relevant, and deliver more value. Measuring to manage and drive results—perfect!

CHAPTER 11

Innovation Interrelationships

For good ideas and true innovation, you need human interaction, conflict, argument, and debate.

—Margaret Heffernan

As a basis for measurements, let's make sure you have winning innovation interrelationships in place—that is, relationships between all parties: your internal relationships between functional departments and leaders, and your external relationships with customers, suppliers, and others you are asking to help innovate. Yes, some of this was covered in Part I *galvanizing*. But it's important to build more on relationships and interactions as we get into measurements. When you begin to measure anything, people start to get nervous. Measurement results can indicate success, but it can also indicate failure to some people, and they don't always take that very well. They believe they will be judged against those metrics (and sometimes they are).

As we get into metrics and measurement of innovation value, I think of a quote from Jeff Thomson, CEO of IMA: "*No measures, no dialogue.*" What Jeff was saying was that if you don't use measurements, how can you even have discussions around improvements, value creation, or degradation and discuss action steps to take going forward? You can't. So you need to measure, then have debates, just like Margaret Heffernan's quote. If you know debate and conflict are coming, you had better be prepared for it. Be ready to facilitate and have healthy discussions instead of defensive positioning and backpedaling.

ESTABLISH INTERNAL DISCUSSION VENUES

One way to better prepare for these discussions is to make innovation a conversation in multiple business processes and areas. Don't let the innovation conversations be limited to a casual chat on a Friday afternoon or even in a scheduled meeting discussion. It needs to be a part of *all* your conversations and business processes. That sounds nice—"Talk innovation in all meetings"—but of course, it's harder to actually execute. So let's get specific.

Consider some of your existing processes, meetings, and management reviews. The next few sections will describe common meeting types that almost every company like conduct already. You might already have direct responsibility and accountability for some of them. And you don't need to change or alter the existing process or deliverables from those existing processes (assuming they are functioning well already), but simply consider how you can better facilitate and hold meaningful innovation dialogues in the existing meetings.

> **No measures, no dialogue.**

Think of it as looking at these meetings through an innovation lens or as putting on your innovation hat. Whatever analogy you like, just make innovation discussion part of these existing processes and reviews.

Discussing Innovation during Capital Allocation/Management Reviews

This is one of the easiest, most natural links. How much of your capital plan is allocated to innovation projects and product innovations? You could even segment your capital projects into incremental, distinctive, and breakthrough capital projects (as described in Chapter 5). The projects may not all specifically be innovation projects and funding, but using the same buckets can be helpful. Have a conversation that asks:

> "What percent of resources are we spending on *incremental* improvements (focused on execution of today's value proposition) vs. *distinctive* improvements (e.g., new products, services, markets, major enhancements) vs. *breakthrough* ideas via totally new product lines, cutting-edge technology, or other wildly imaginative new ideas?"

I've been a president of a business and served on multiple executive teams, and I can tell you that this approach leads to a much more stimulating discussion than traditional capital reviews. And you just may be shocked at how much is going into that incremental bucket and how it is squeezing out many distinctive and breakthrough projects that should be considered for funding.

Discussing Innovation during Business/Strategic Planning Meetings

This is another obvious and easy fit. As you evaluate turbulence in your market, assess customer needs, review your value proposition, and assess core competencies, identify the areas in which you need to innovate or reinvent products or processes. One business I worked with used the term "overlay initiatives" to define what the business could look like if it made significant investments, had changes in strategy (i.e., overlays on the existing business), and what the future state would look like.

Changes in strategy can certainly be innovative, so focus those conversations on where you want to make strategy changes, where you want to keep or accelerate strategies, and what the associated innovation needs will be in those areas. Again, simply using the lexicon of incremental, distinctive, and breakthrough to describe your strategic thrusts in a plan is helpful in articulating to the other executives the scope, size, and timing of a strategy and its impact on your business.

Discussing Innovation during Budgeting Sessions

Today, you likely challenge mid-level managers to be responsible for budgets and create operating plans for the year—this is a fairly common business practice. When they put budgets together, do they allow for unexpected surprises and opportunities where they could innovate or need to innovate during the upcoming period? What is your mechanism to handle unfunded opportunities? Do you do that at a top-line level and grant exceptions, or do you keep a pool of funds for opportunities that arise after budget finalization? Almost every CFO struggles with this.

You need to be "closest to the pin" (to use a golf analogy) with your estimates and budgets. You likely can't keep slush funds or earmark pools of monies for discretion later, but inevitably you need to do that very thing. To simply say NO to an opportunity that comes up during the year because it wasn't in the budget is poor leadership and poor management. However you handle this in your company, just be clear on how to get funding for opportunities that will inevitably occur during the year, likely from innovation mechanisms that can add value and simply can't wait for a new budget cycle.

Where should you invest your cash in value-creating innovation scenarios vs. holding it? One of the research insights from Clay Christensen's "The Capitalist's Dilemma" points to a contributor who said, "*We've lost the concept of having a portfolio of business. Out of every business, we expect incremental improvement on these key financial metrics.*" The respondent thought this loss of a portfolio mentality with a range of investments produced a crowded, efficiency-focused near-term agenda.

Your challenge then in innovation governance is to ensure that you have a balanced range of efforts with which you are experimenting, funding, executing, and measuring multiple innovation projects and ideas. Innovation governance is managing a portfolio of business initiatives to drive value. Monitoring execution, challenging strategy and results, making course corrections, investing additional funds—all of these activities are likely happening in your business today; apply a lens of innovation to those activities.

Discussing Innovation during Operations Management Meetings

Many companies have a monthly meeting about operational results from the prior month. It usually occurs after the books are closed for the month, and leadership wants to understand the good, the bad, and the ugly of the results. These monthly ops reviews are typically about results, not necessarily innovation. But, ops is in a constant state of problem solving to drive results. They likely have some of your best problem solving people within the business.

How can you include innovation in these reviews and discussions to better harness that problem-solving skill set to drive more company-wide innovation? In the same way you want everyone on the front line to be responsible for quality products and services and on-time delivery to the customer, make sure they are keeping innovation top of mind and are always looking for ways to add more value through efficiencies or to the customer directly.

Discussing Innovation during Enterprise Risk Management Reviews

What does innovation have to do with an Enterprise Risk Management (ERM) review? Isn't that the antithesis of innovation? Again, go back to the concept of innovation governance, where two seemingly opposite forces are actually complementary. Think about what you normally do in an ERM review. You work to identify the inherit risks that you face in your business, and then consider the controls you can put in place to minimize those risks. The result is a lower residual risk level that meets your risk tolerance level. However, there is another step you can take in this business process. Ask yourself when looking at these risks—"If we could take an identified risk and solve for the inherit exposure that it creates, could this be something that we could do better than anyone else (competitors)? And could that actually be a differentiation factor in our value proposition?" Think about it. If you have inherent risk in your business environment, it's likely that your competitors have the same inherent risk. If you can solve for it and they can't, that's differentiation that you need to tell your clients and prospects about! In your next risk management or ERM review, consider where some of your risks may lead to an opportunity to turn it into a point of distinction and differentiation for your value proposition.

Chapter 13 will get deep into specific metrics and measurements, but for now, consider some of the questions you should be asking in these business processes that would help your overall view and action planning in relation to innovation efforts:

1. *Budgeting process*: What are the dollars allocated to running the ongoing current business vs. new development opportunities?

2. *Capital process*: Reviewing the percent allocation by product life-cycle stage, is your portfolio balanced? Are you investing only in mature, startup, or declining products? What's in the pipeline?

3. *Innovation process*: What is the percent split of funds to incremental, distinctive, breakthrough projects? What kind of balance do you have, and do you have an imbalance in a manner that matches your overall business strategy?

4. *Customer feedback*: What is your ROI for increased revenue or customer retention initiatives? Are you getting feedback from customers and investing dollars that will drive retention, loyalty, satisfaction, and overall value?

> **88% of research participants identified the need to better link innovation into strategic planning discussions.**

5. *Operations reviews*: What are your on-time delivery, quality, and returns figures? As you monitor these metrics, should you be investing in projects/initiatives to improve these metrics? Will your customers see this as value added, and what kind of return will you get for this?

6. *ERM reviews*: Where do you mitigate great risk and exposure in your business processes and overall risk landscape? Do you do that better than the competition, and can you offer this as a distinguishing factor? Consider looking at the standard deviation or absolute values of inherent vs. residual risk levels.

When you look at all of these business processes holistically, you are collectively managing risks and opportunities. In its innovation findings, APQC highlighted this point:

> *"Organizations should be deliberate in how they allocate resources depending on the amount of risk involved."*[22]

And in a separate study on innovation collaboration, APQC noted the need to *"integrate and align the open innovation process with other relevant processes to ensure key entities are involved at critical points."*[23] This can be internal or external. Rather than have a separate innovation process or evaluation, simply include those conversations in your existing business processes—where do you want to take risk and drive innovation to create value? In the same study, APQC also noted that *"Knowledge and change management techniques facilitate the embedding of innovation."*[24] Think of knowledge and change management as a normal course of business, not something new just for innovation.

If you have innovation conversations in these existing business processes, many of which the finance and accounting leader already owns, you create more "staying power" around innovation and overall value creation because you will find more people in more venues across the company talking about innovation, the impact on innovation, the value of innovation, the priority of innovation, and so on. Make it a part of everyday language and management in your business. The IMA research confirms this and points to the need to integrate innovation into the planning and budgeting process and then track and measure innovation results.

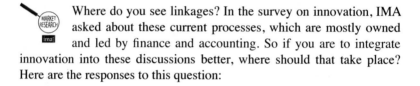 Where do you see linkages? In the survey on innovation, IMA asked about these current processes, which are mostly owned and led by finance and accounting. So if you are to integrate innovation into these discussions better, where should that take place? Here are the responses to this question:

- 69% said to incorporate innovation discussions into *budgeting*.

- 64% said to incorporate innovation discussions into *capital Planning*.

- 69% said to incorporate innovation discussions into *operational Reviews*.

- 88% said to incorporate innovation discussions into *strategic planning* (including risk and opportunity identification)!

The short answer here is that the majority see opportunity and value in holding innovation dialogue in *existing* business processes. Why create more, additional venues for discussion when you have good forums that already exist? And these are forums and discussions you either lead directly or are a key participant in already. There is no need for a new steering committee or a new "innovation meeting." Much of the needed structure exists today, and it's a matter of integrating innovation discussion into those forums.

ESTABLISH EXTERNAL INNOVATION DISCUSSIONS

As you consider the innovation channels discussed in Chapters 6–10, you will likely reach outside your organization for innovation support and value creation at some point. You can use those innovation channels to do this, but if you already have several ways to get feedback from outside constituents, you can use those to set the stage for innovation dialogue. Think about how you can prepare for that conversation of creating joint innovation value when you are in the midst of these existing connection points.

Annual Customer Satisfaction Surveys

Hopefully you use some sort of mechanism to collect and evaluate customer satisfaction feedback. There are many ways to capture this, whether by a simple Net Promoter Score on a phone call or via an annual survey asking for feedback. Whatever the process, use that opportunity to ask about innovation and the kinds of ideas on the minds of your customers. You don't even have to use the word "innovation" itself. You might simply ask your customers what they would they like to see in your value proposition that would be important to them.

Annual Supplier Reviews

I've seen both ends of the spectrum when it comes to annual supplier reviews. I've seen the draconian sessions where it is simply about beating up the vendor (not "supplier," because that suggests there is some sort of partnership or relationship) for pure cost savings and threatening to move your business unless they lower their commodity prices. The other end of the spectrum is a real partnership meeting where you and the supplier look at your value proposition and see if there is something they can do differently with what they supply to help improve the overall value proposition to the end customer. It's this latter conversation that can lead to a good discussion around innovation. You can work together to "make the pie bigger for everyone" rather than "re-slice who gets how much of the pie." This pie concept is important. Rather than assume that the pie is fixed, that it's a matter of how it gets divided up in your market, industry, and value chain, you can look at the pie as being something that can be expanded and grow larger for everyone—more opportunity and more value for everyone. I don't know if you can always grow the pie, but I challenge you to think of more ways to grow the pie rather than focusing on how to split it up!

You probably have other mechanisms and opportunities to solicit input and feedback from customers, suppliers, and other partners. If you can introduce—and keep having—innovation discussions in these various venues and reviews, you will deepen, strengthen, and broaden your overall innovation discussion and hopefully set up that constituent for a deeper innovation partnership in the future.

SOWING THE SEEDS TO SUCCESSFUL INNOVATION INTERRELATIONSHIPS

To conclude this chapter, I want to use a farming analogy as an example of what you need to do with your interrelationships to support innovation. Crop farming is pretty straightforward—not easy, mind you, but straightforward. You plow the ground, you plant the seeds, you nurture the plant growth with fertilizer, water, and weed control, and you eventually harvest the crop.

Building successful relationships that will foster innovation requires the same approach. You can't just call in a supplier and expect to be in the "harvest" stage. You need to work the ground and set the stage, you need to plant the seed and let them know you are open to their ideas and to working together, and you need to nurture those ideas together before you can harvest and reap the benefits.

Yes, this sounds rather simplistic and a no-brainer, but you'd be surprised how many people don't lay the groundwork for success. You have to develop these relationships in order to benefit from them. It does take time, but it is time well spent. Consider ways of doing a better job of planting and fertilizing so those partners are more responsive and helpful in working with you on your business's value proposition and ultimately creating more value in the future.

Finally, ask yourself (and your fellow senior managers) these questions to ensure you're on the right track to success:

- Do you have innovation efforts engrained in your normal course of business?

- Do you have alignment and balance in your innovation agenda?

- Are you effectively managing change?

- Do you have the right metrics in place (see Chapter 13)?

These are good rules and good questions to operate under and ponder. How would you judge that you and your business operate under these rules, and how would you respond to these questions? Some of this setup should have been addressed via galvanizing the organization, but in this discussion of interrelationships, these questions and "innovation rules" are more directed to how you are managing the entirety of the portfolio and acting collectively as a business.

Now that you've identified the interrelationships to help incorporate innovation into the regular conversations both within the organization and externally, the next stage of measuring involves balanced scorecarding specifically for innovation measurement and management.

CHAPTER 12

The Balanced Scorecard—For Innovation

Intelligence is the ability to adapt to change.
—Stephen Hawking

The balanced scorecard (BSC) was a profound work back in the early 1990s. Today it's hard to find a business that doesn't use some sort of BSC format or framework to measure results. The BSC isn't a complicated concept, but there are several components to it. You need to have a strategy map, search for lead indicators to predict lagging measures, understand causal relationships, and find balance. That last part, find balance, is critical. The heart of the concept is to use multiple metrics to measure the success and value of your business. You use a balance of metrics that isn't just financial in nature (which are mostly lag indicators) but that also measure results and monitor leading indicators in the categories of:

- *Financial*
- *Customer*
- *Internal business processes*
- *Learning and growth*

The causal relationships go from the bottom up—that is, what you do and measure in *learning and growth* feeds what you need to do in *internal business processes*. That in turn provides what you can deliver to *customers*, which generates value and produces lag metrics in the *financial* category. That's a bit oversimplified, but the 30-second version of the balanced scorecard makes a lot of sense to many people. We all want to create value by attaining our mission and fulfilling our vision. That value creation comes in different forms and can be measured in a multitude of ways. The BSC framework helps you formulate that measurement system and manage your business.

Measuring innovation and innovation value created poses a similar yet slightly different challenge. It's similar in that it is difficult to measure innovation value, like business value, and it takes a variety of metrics to measure results and be able to monitor leading indicators around innovation. There is a need for a dashboard and measurement system for innovation, and that is what I have created via innovation governance and the Innovation Value Score® (IVS) body of work that will be described in detail in Chapter 13.

> **IVS creates a dialogue around innovation value creation—where should we take actions?**

I applied a BSC framework with which to measure innovation. This can be done simply enough, but do you need to go further? That is, the BSC concept makes recommendations to metrics that you could use within your scorecard, but it does not go so far as to prescribe specific metrics that you must use in your scorecard. It's up to the practitioner to decide what those metrics are. This makes sense because different businesses, with different strategies, and in different industries need to measure some things the same but other things differently. The approach for innovation measurement is similar in that people tend to use a variety of measurements to talk about innovation, therefore making any comparison between companies, markets, and industries is next to impossible. Does that matter? I think it does, and the research showed that comparability is critical.

Therefore, a common framework and model are needed to measure basic innovation in all companies; then it will be possible to establish what "good, better, and best" measures look like and compare innovation within and outside of various industries, different geographical regions, and in different company sizes and structures. The end result is a meaningful discussion around innovation value creation and how you can achieve more.

INNOVATION VALUE SCORE®

Innovation Value Score (IVS) is a tool you can use to measure innovation value at a directional level and create a dialogue around innovation value creation. Chapter 13 will get to the details of IVS—what makes it up, how to calculate it, and how to take meaningful actions from the results. This chapter lays out the framework that outlines IVS measurement and calculation, then describes the similarities and differences between standard BSC principles and the principles of IVS. The basic construct and rationale has many similarities, which makes it easy for finance and accounting professionals to grasp and implement IVS quickly.

WHY MODEL IVS AFTER THE BSC?

The BSC was created as a way to measure and manage a business. It is intended to be a measurement and management system, not a singular calculation and end point. IVS has the same goal—to be a system used to manage a business's entire innovation value creation agenda, not just to calculate a result and move onto the next task. This speaks to the chapter's opening quote by Stephen Hawking. The intelligence of IVS is not in simply calculating the results, it is in how you interpret those calculations and turn that information into intelligence to drive change and value in your business. Having that intelligence paired with the guts and desire to take action and to adapt will lead to increased value.

Additionally, if you believe that innovation governance belongs in the office of the CFO and that senior finance and accounting professionals should be leaders in innovation governance, then why not choose a tool and methodology that you are already familiar with and that is rather universally accepted? You can utilize a baseline BSC framework and modify it to measure and manage for innovation value. There is less value and more time involved in learning an entirely new methodology, debating it, and gaining acceptance. Why go through that when there is something great already in the finance toolbox that can be adjusted to serve your needs in innovation measurement and management and in overall innovation governance?

Similarities between IVS and the BSC

IVS uses a BSC construct and a fairly traditional BSC model of the four categories and causal relationships. Specifically, IVS looks like a BSC model in the following similar characteristics:

- IVS uses four traditional, although slightly modified, categories of measures in the areas of customer, growth, operational excellence, and financial.

  IVS stresses a balanced approach to measuring innovation value— you need to have metrics for each of the four categories—but the balance among those categories will be different depending on your strategic business intent. (See the discussion on business archetypes in Chapter 13.)

- IVS does not use weightings in calculations. Therefore, no category has more significance than others, and weightings aren't applied in the calculations.

- Lagging indicators (results) are important, but leading indicators, or milestone marks, on how innovation is advancing are important to predict results, facilitate go/no-go decision making, and drive discussion on where improvements can be made. IVS uses both leading and lagging indicators, and at least one of the reports provided focuses on the review of leading indicators as a place to take actions to get better lag results.

- IVS results should have improvement targets for future periods, and there should be associated budgets and initiatives tied to the metrics that will lead to the desired results.

- Benchmarks are useful in setting budget goals and targets for future results. Benchmarks can be minimum levels or aspirational goals depending on the metric, industry, demographics, and so on. They are invaluable in considering what your measurement results could be and should be as you develop and deliver your specific value proposition in your market.

Differences between IVS and the BSC

Where IVS differs from the BSC is in its characteristics that are specific to innovation and trying to account for other related factors to enable comparability discussions. The differences include:

- IVS has similar categories of metrics, but the categorical ordering and causal relationships are slightly different when you are looking specifically at innovation. IVS begins with the customer perspective because the goal is to drive innovation value and better your value proposition. If there is no customer, there is no business. So your innovation roadmap should be governed by the innovation value you can create for your customer. I have found that starting with the customer leads to the best mind-set of focused innovation to drive value, rather than innovating for the sake of innovation and focusing on activity only.

- IVS calculates a categorical score in each of the four categories. Therefore, the individual metrics are normalized by assigned values on a scale of 1 to 10. These are then averaged together to create a categorical score in each IVS category. Looking at the standard deviation within an IVS category can be important as you look for balance across measures and consistency in category results. You will inevitably have some metrics where you will shine and others that will be lower, but there should be minimal levels and expectations for how low some metrics should be—hence the rationale of looking at standard deviation within the groups and in total. Closing the gap, or reducing the standard deviation, especially in your most critical IVS category, should be a focus.

- IVS also includes an overall score made up of the scores of all the individual metrics. IMPORTANT NOTE: Calculating the overall IVS score is not the be all and end all of measurement. The individual components that make up the composite score are far more important because they provide value in identifying areas that create innovation value and in clarifying areas that need improvement. But the overall IVS composite score does enable you to have a relative conversation on innovation value creation from company to company, industry to industry, geography to geography, and so on. This makes it possible to gauge how you are excelling, where you are struggling, and where you can apply lessons learned from others.

- The metrics for IVS are predefined. Unlike the BSC model, which offers examples but doesn't prescribe metrics, IVS prescribes metrics. Yes, by doing so, some businesses will relate more (or less) to some metrics than others. And, no, it isn't ideal to do this. But defining the metrics provides a common yardstick with which to discuss innovation and have some comparability.

To compensate for this, there are 24 metrics overall—six in each category—and you can select a minimum of four in each category when you calculate your IVS. So you don't have to use a particular metric if you feel it isn't as relevant to your business or industry or if you don't collect the data to calculate it. While this allows a minimal level of flexibility, you lose comparability, which is a key desire.

At the end of the day, you can rationalize away why your IVS score may be lower than you want (or higher than you deserve), but it is meant to be a directionally correct metric that stimulates conversation and points to actions to take to drive value. So argue away! Let's have fierce conversations on creating innovation value!!! If you can do that, then you can move ahead!

THE DIMENSIONALITY OF INNOVATION VALUE SCORE

Aside from the BSC categorical views, IVS information also includes some other "cuts" or dimensions. Each of the 24 metrics is delineated by the following dimensions:

- *Incremental, distinctive, or breakthrough*

- *Inputs, processes, or results*

- *Leading or lagging indicators*

This is further information for looking at your results via the metrics and slicing through the information for valuable insights. Looking at the four categories of IVS scores is important. But so is looking at your balance of incremental vs. distinctive vs. breakthrough metric results, as discussed in Chapter 5.

Another valuable cut is looking at your corresponding metric results for inputs, processes, and results so you can assess points of goodness and areas of improvement. These cuts all provide different views of balance or imbalance, as the case may be. You may want to have imbalance in some areas, (e.g., more results, inputs, and initiatives on distinctive areas vs. incremental areas if you are trying to dramatically improve your value proposition), but you want the metrics to be measuring this so that you can manage it.

Measurement in innovation needs to be systemic and holistic, not a single measure. You need to be able to ask multiple questions, to have multiple cuts of your measurement data, and to have discussions around results and goals.

THIS METRIC DOESN'T WORK FOR ME BECAUSE...

> **See the forest for the trees— use metrics to ensure your innovation actions create value.**

No, some of the metrics may not apply 100% to your business. No, some of the benchmarks may be too high for you in your given industry. No, a metric may be more incremental than distinctive, more distinctive than breakthrough. No, not all of the metric input information is easy to get. But keep this in mind—the goal is a common baseline, a directionally correct measurement and management system to measure innovation and take actionable steps to drive improvement.

Yes, it undoubtedly will not be perfect, but, *yes*, the value in having the dialogue and taking the actions far outweigh any mismatches in specific measures or benchmark levels. Don't get caught up in the perfection of calculations and results; take that energy and apply it to healthy debate and execution of improvements to drive innovation value in your business. Use the data, evaluate the various cuts of information, and make decisions on how to achieve more innovation value. Find ways to get to *yes*—and to get to *value*!

INNOVATION IS A TEAM SPORT

I have mentioned a couple of times already that innovation is a team sport. You can definitely see that in how IVS measures innovation results. When some people talk about innovation, they quickly go to technology and product development. But collectively we have to have innovation conversations that are more encompassing—conversations that not only talk about *breakthrough* technologies and new products, but also *incremental* and *distinctive* innovations around and within your existing value proposition, all of which drive value to your customers. Because you know by now that you probably shouldn't be doing it if it isn't driving value to the customer.

Some of the metrics you look at in IVS are directly related to innovation value creation. Others are more indirect and support the business strategy as a whole. Metrics and gauges on dashboards all have uses and functionality, and some are more critical and telling than others. Some of the metrics are not pure innovation metrics, but they're absolutely related and part of the entire *management system* around managing innovation value.

Look at the IVS metrics individually *and* as a whole. When you look at them as a whole, are you getting the results and value creation you want for your business at this point in time and according to the strategies you are employing? This is the critical question for debate.

Lastly, embrace the use of a BSC framework to measure innovation. You may even have a scorecard system or process in place already that gets to several or many of these metrics. If you do, fantastic! You are a step closer to having a system to measure and manage innovation value as well.

But don't stop at using a traditional BSC alone to measure innovation. Apply the other dimensionality of IVS to enable deeper, more comprehensive innovation discussions in your business. And if you choose to use the IVS framework, look at the associated benchmarks for each measure and at how other companies, both similar to and different from you, achieve results. Ask yourself: What should our results be, and what should we be striving for to maximize our value proposition?

In the concluding chapter about measuring, the third element in your Innovation Elixir, it's time to get into the details of IVS. We've seen how it relates to the BSC as an underlying framework, and you should have a better picture of how it differs and why.

So as you look at the measures, benchmarks, underlying rationale, and the encompassing system in the next chapter, keep in mind the idea of "Not seeing the forest for the trees." The old adage means that when you are looking too closely at any one part, you are likely to miss the bigger picture and meaning. Certainly, pay attention to the detail in the following chapter. But do it mindfully—review and interpret that detail and keep framing it in the larger picture of a total measurement and management system for innovation value creation. The individual details are important, but not as important as the overall system—see the forest!

CHAPTER 13

Innovation Value Score®

*Innovation is the specific instrument of entrepreneurship.
It is the act that endows resources with a new capacity to
create wealth.*

—Peter Drucker

Calculating your IVS is only the beginning of understanding your innovation value and success, *not the end point*. Remember the images you painted in your mind in the introduction to Part IV?

Measurement enables dialogue and can help you make decisions and get more and better results. The measure element in innovation is iterative and ongoing. Measurement is a constant stride for balance, improvement, and value creation within your innovation governance framework.

IVS is about more than measurement—it is also about overall innovation value creation and management. But through measurement, you gain insight. With that insight, you can have dialogue and discussion about where you may want to invest or divest, where you want to make changes to your business strategy or execution, and how you want to adapt to the future and achieve your mission and visions.

You can and should think of calculating your IVS akin to Frederick Taylor's time-and-motion studies. Did they perform time-and-motion studies to get a measure and then go home and call it a day? No, they performed the studies to get a baseline of results and then looked for ways to improve. This should be your ultimate innovation measurement goal: Get a baseline and improve the results.

As you can imagine, I was very deliberate in what I called this system for innovation. In the end, it comes down to value. What kind of value are you creating for customers and other stakeholders? I don't think it's as simple as a pure market value multiple or market value calculation; it's more complex than that, and the end goal is measuring value from many aspects, both internal and external—just as the quote from Peter Drucker describes.

A market-value calculation doesn't give you anything to work with. What actions can you take from that calculation to specifically improve your results and value creation? Also, keep in mind that not all innovation needs to be breakthrough, but innovation efforts all do need to share one common mantra—*to create value!*

> **This should be your ultimate innovation measurement goal: Get a baseline and then improve the results.**

It is quite a challenge to measure innovation; here's one approach to what an "ideal metric" would need to measure:

"*The ideal metric must allow you to assess growth for the future. The one that will enable (and ennoble) leaders to make the best long-term decisions for sustained growth and innovation without displeasing investors. Both leaders and investors need a cognitive baptism to the idea that growth doesn't come from efficiency.*"[25]

Efficiency can create some value. And depending on your strategy map and current positioning, that currently may be your company's biggest area of value creation. But that value creation strategy isn't sustainable in the long term. Sooner or later, the lemon has been squeezed, and all the juice is extracted. You can focus on efficiencies, but it is only one part of your innovation governance leadership. Neither can a metric only be about disruptive innovation efforts or new market growth. There really is no one-size-fits-all singular metric for all businesses that are executing differing strategies. Thus, the need is for a blended metric and thoughtful approach to discern the calculated results.

FOUR CATEGORIES OF INNOVATION VALUE

Chapter 12 discussed using the BSC framework as the base for measuring innovation value. As I said then, you can argue over the fairness of specific metrics or their applicability to a particular industry or company, but it's better to spend the time improving and learning instead of debating exactitudes. That will create value. Arguing only produces heartache. Within the IVS construct are four slightly altered BSC categories that are reordered to facilitate a discussion specifically around innovation:

1. Customer
2. Growth
3. Operational excellence
4. Financial

Kaplan and Norton were very deliberate in their ordering of the categories in the BSC and the causal relationships that would occur. I understand, support, and respect this ordering. When using this BSC framework specifically for innovation measurement, however, I believe a slight modification is needed, starting with the customer. Let's take a closer look at each of these categories in a bit more detail.

#1: Customer Innovation

Whether you begin with an internally focused view on what you believe the customer wants or literally talk to your customers about their wants and needs—both are appropriate and good places to start creating innovation value and measuring results. Why are you in business? To serve your customers. Everyone has customers. You may call them something different—clients, constituents, members, and so on—but you serve someone with your value proposition. Your organization exists to provide value to others. Once you have your measures in place in this category, you then move on to the category of growth.

#2: Growth Innovation

The growth category is where you would expect to see many of the more commonly mentioned innovation metrics. Depending on what's happening with your customer metrics, you will take causal actions in the growth category. If your customers are unhappy with your products, should you be developing new ones? Should you be getting into new markets? There are many questions to ask, and many metrics you can put in place to facilitate the dialogue.

#3: Operational Excellence Innovation

If the growth category primarily addressed the "what" you are providing to your customers and your strategy of getting there, the operational excellence category is definitely about "how." Forget about the future for a second—if you don't deliver today, you won't be around for the future!

In the operational excellence category, who cares whether you call it continuous process improvement or incremental innovation? Just do it! You can watch metrics in this category and ask if you should be changing how you are executing on your value proposition and how you can achieve the mantra of "better, cheaper, faster." This category is all about what you are delivering *today*.

#4: Financial Innovation

Yes, financial measures are mostly lag results. They are the fruits of your labor that you sow into the other categories. They are important measures that you will use to make decisions and provide feedback to other areas of your business, customers, and the market in general. If your business archetype (discussed later in this chapter) involves having a propriety market position, you may have your strongest measures and make many of your decisions based on this category.

In sum, there are four categories of measures to review and discuss; look at the causal relationships among those measures and what you need to do to drive more value. You can look at the measures independently, but looking at them holistically should paint a picture of your business strategy success and areas for improvement.

IVS METRICS

Next, let's look at the specific metrics that have been selected in each IVS category. I could write another whole book on the metrics I didn't select and why, but let's focus on the ones that were selected and the value you can get from monitoring and measuring them.

I selected 24 metrics that can be used to holistically measure innovation value creation in your business. When you enter your data for calculation and actionable reporting in the actual IVS software platform, you need to only choose a minimum of four metrics in each of the four categories—a total of 16 total metrics. This allows you to skip specific metrics if you feel they don't apply to your business or industry or if you don't capture the data to calculate the metrics. But these 24 metrics were painstakingly chosen to form a measurement and management system around innovation value creation that would create a deeper level of discussion and debate on strategy and actionability so businesses can move forward and drive more value creation.

Exhibit 13-1 contains a list of the 24 metrics as well as some of the major characteristics for each.

Seeing that list, you might realize that you already measure some of these metrics and wonder what makes them innovation metrics. That's a great question. My response: Innovation measures should reflect your business in part through normal, existing measures. Innovation measurement is not just about special innovation activity. When it's done right and creates real business value, you should be able to measure that value with existing, maybe slightly augmented metrics from what you use today. So while some of these metrics may be similar to things your measure today, look at them as a whole and how they collectively tell you a story on innovation

Exhibit 13-1

Innovation Value Score®

	Metric	IVS Category	Lead Lag	Input Process Result	Incremental Distinctive Breakthrough
1	Net Promotor Score	Customer Value	Lag	Result	Distinctive
2	Customer Retention	Customer Value	Lag	Result	Incremental
3	% External Ideation	Customer Value	Lead	Process	Distinctive
4	CRM Strength	Customer Value	Lead	Process	Distinctive
5	% of New Customers	Customer Value	Lead	Result	Distinctive
6	% of Strategic Accounts	Customer Value	Lead	Result	Distinctive
7	Market/Product Exits	Financial	Lag	Process	Distinctive
8	Gross Margin Improvement	Financial	Lag	Process	Incremental
9	% Revenue from New Products	Financial	Lag	Result	Distinctive
10	Return on Assets	Financial	Lag	Result	Distinctive
11	Free Cash Flow	Financial	Lead	Input	Breakthrough
12	% Capital to Revenue	Financial	Lead	Input	Distinctive
13	Brand Awareness	Growth & Advancement	Lead	Input	Distinctive
14	# of New patents, trademarks, licenses	Growth & Advancement	Lead	Process	Breakthrough
15	Innovation Pipeline	Growth & Advancement	Lead	Process	Distinctive
16	Speed to Market	Growth & Advancement	Lead	Process	Distinctive
17	# of New Markets over 3 years	Growth & Advancement	Lead	Result	Breakthrough
18	# of New Products over 3 years	Growth & Advancement	Lead	Result	Distinctive
19	Quality - Returns	Ops Excellence & People	Lag	Process	Incremental
20	Supplier value generated	Ops Excellence & People	Lag	Process	Incremental
21	On Time Delivery	Ops Excellence & People	Lag	Process	Incremental
22	Employee Engagement %	Ops Excellence & People	Lead	Input	Distinctive
23	Employee Retention	Ops Excellence & People	Lead	Input	Incremental
24	Training dollars per employee	Ops Excellence & People	Lead	Input	Incremental
	Stats -->	6 per category; 4 minimum for calculation	Lag - 9 Lead - 15	Input - 6 Process - 10 Result - 8	Incremental - 7 Distinctive - 14 Breakthrough - 3

value creation and point to areas for strategic imperatives to drive more value.

Exhibit 13-2 provides another summary view of the metrics. This one is an illustrative IVS Summary Scorecard. You can begin to see how the metrics work in a scorecarding context. As you look at the exhibit, pause for a moment and reflect on these measures and their applicability. Consider how you envision each one of these metrics supporting your own innovation agenda and giving you information with which to further evaluate, monitor, and take actions to increase your levels of innovation value. Imagine discussing the results of these metrics in all forums, as discussed in Chapter 11.

When you calculate a particular metric, the IVS platform then normalizes that metric and converts the result into that measurement's IVS score. This rating, from 1 to 10, is applied so that you can compare and compile all

140   Advancing Innovation

Exhibit 13-2

Innovation Value Score®

		Metric IVS	Category IVS	Category Std Dev
Company Size:	$5M - 100M			
Company Type:	Non-Profit			
Geo Region:	Canada			
Market Segment:	Manufacturing			
Self Assessed Archetype:	Customized Solutions Provider			
Customer Value {Custom Solution Provider}	Net Promotor Score	9	4.8	2.7
	Customer Retention	5		
	New Customers	2		
	Strategic Accounts	3		
	CRM Strength	4		
	External Ideation	6		
Growth & Advancement {Product Developer}	New Products over 3 years	2	5.4	3.3
	New Markets over 3 years	9		
	New patents, trademarks, licenses	9		
	Innovation Pipeline	2		
	Brand Awareness	5		
	Speed to Market	5		
Operational Excellence & People {Best Price/Low Cost Leader}	On Time Delivery	7	4.2	2.1
	Employee Retention	4		
	Employee Engagement	4		
	Training dollars per employee	5		
	Quality - Returns	4		
	Supplier value generated	1		
Financial {Proprietary Leader}	Revenue from New Products	6	5.7	2.3
	Capital to Revenue	6		
	Gross Margin Improvement	2		
	Free Cash Flow	4		
	Return on Assets	8		
	Market/Product Exits	7		
Overall Innovation Value Score		**5.0**		
Standard Deviation of all IVS metrics / Category IVS scores		2.5	0.6	

the differing types of metrics into a normalized, comparable form. The 1 to 10 ratings for each metric are shown in the following pages and are embedded into the IVS calculations engine. These ratings fall into four categories, shown in Exhibit 13-3.

Finally, as you review the metrics and their associated benchmarks, you will find two distinctive sets of benchmarks, each representing half the metrics.

The first set comprises benchmarks that have been applied directly from experience and some best-in-class data points. These metrics tend to be

Exhibit 13-3: IVS Metrics Ratings Categories

IVS Scores	Metric level definition
10	Elite performers, the best 10%
7–9	Top performers—growth/advancing business level
4–6	Median performers—sustaining/maintaining, but potentially slipping in areas
0–3	Bottom performers—harvest/shrinking level

harder to measure or are metrics that are less mainstream and more difficult to get enough data for comparison to other metrics at this time.

The second set contains benchmarks that have been provided by APQC from its Open Standards Benchmarking database. I am pleased to work with APQC in providing and utilizing these benchmarks to aid in your calculation and measurement related to innovation value. If you are not familiar with APQC, it describes itself as:

> "APQC helps organizations work smarter, faster, and with greater confidence. It is the world's foremost authority in benchmarking, best practices, process and performance improvement, and knowledge management. APQC's unique structure as a member-based nonprofit makes it a differentiator in the marketplace. APQC partners with more than 500 member organizations worldwide in all industries. With more than 35 years of experience, APQC remains the world's leader in transforming organizations."

APQC has more than 500 member organizations from 48 countries. The data it provided for these IVS benchmarks comes from many industries, geographies, and various sizes of corporations. Exhibit 13-4 shows the associated demographics that represent how these benchmarks were arrived at. You'll find a mix of 22 industries from around the world that are a variety of sizes, from revenues of less than $100 million to greater than $20 billion.

Now for a detailed view of the 24 metrics. This information includes definitions, descriptions, formulas, benchmarks, and, ultimately, the reasons why these metrics were chosen to be a part of this innovation measurement and management system. APQC has provided benchmarks on half of the metrics, and those benchmarks delineate elite performers (top 10%), Top Performers (top 25%), Median, and Bottom Performers.

Exhibit 13-4: APQC demographics *(N = 5511)* for APQC Benchmarks provided in IVS scores.

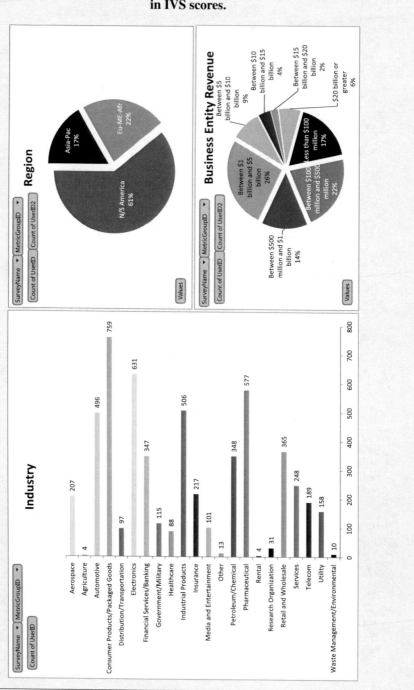

Exhibit 13-5

			Input	Incremental
		Lead	Process	Distinctive
		Lag	Result	Breakthrough

Metric Name: Net Promoter Score

| **IVS Category:** | Customer | | Lag | Result | Distinctive |

Definition: Percentage of customers who are Promoters minus the percentage who are Detractors. Your organization's Net Promoter Score is calculated based on surveys of your customers - answers to the question: How likely is it that you would recommend [this organization] to a friend or colleague? Respondents can answer with any number from 0 to 10, where 0 = not at all likely, 5 = neutral, 10 = extremely likely. To calculate your NPS, take the percentage of customers who are Promoters (score 9-10) and subtract the percentage who are Detractors (score 0-6)

Innovation Significance: If you start with Customer Value as your first category in IVS calculations - Net Promoter Score is a key metric to determining if customers are happy and you are generating value for them which is especially critical for companies with a customer solutions archetype.

Inputs & Formula:	Direct input metric. Percentage of customers who are Promoters minus the percentage who are Detractors.	Units %	**Comments** This information is likely captured via a call center process and the result can be entered directly into IVS. Range of values are -100% (all Detractors) to 100% (all promoters)

Related Metrics: Customer Satisfaction, Customer Retention, Customer Loyalty, Growth

APQC.

APQC or General Best Practice Benchmarks

IVS Score Normalization:			
	35+%	10	Top 10% of Companies
	33-35%	9	
	30-33%	8	75% Quartile
	28-30%	7	
	25-28%	6	
	22-25%	5	50% Quartile
	20-22%	4	
	18-20%	3	
	15-18%	2	25% Quartile
	10-15%	1	
	< 10%	0	Below 25% Quartile

Future Analysis, Benchmarking, Insights and Assumptions:
(we continue to research and develop additional data points, trends and benchmarks)

Business Strategy Archetype:	Strongest archetype tends to be = Customized Solutions Provider. These businesses tend to have the best NPS results, likely followed by Product Developers who please customers with new products and focus less on cost efficiencies.
Industries to Watch:	Retails businesses tend to be the most versed in NPS measurement and management and skilled in driving customer satisfaction via sophisticated internal programs.
Relevance of Company Size:	Company size does not play a significant role, but larger companies do tend to more frequently track NPS and have internal programs, training and tracking systems to drive to higher levels of satisfaction.

Exhibit 13-6

		Input	Incremental
	Lead	Process	Distinctive
	Lag	Result	Breakthrough

INNOVATION
VALUE SCORE™

Metric Name: Customer Retention

IVS Category: Customer

	Lag	Result	Incremental

Definition: The customer retention rate is defined as the number of customers who were active three years ago and are still active, divided by the number of customers who were active three years ago.

Innovation Significance: Customers will not stay with you if you are not providing them value - continuous value and value that is incrementally and distinctively being added to over time.

		Units	Comments
Inputs & Formula:	The number of customers who were active three years ago and are still active, divided by the number of customers who were active three years ago, multiplied by 100%	%	Calculate the number of customers remaining at the end of the period without counting the number of new customers acquired to calculate current customer retention. Active Customer are customers who have purchased a business's products at least once in a 12-month period.

Related Metrics: Customer Satisfaction, Customer Retention, Customer Loyalty, Growth

APQC.

APQC or General Best Practice Benchmarks

IVS Score Normalization:

98 +%	10	Top 10% of Companies
97-98%	9	
95-97%	8	75% Quartile
93-95%	7	
90-93%	6	
88-90%	5	50% Quartile
85-88%	4	
79-85%	3	
73-78%	2	25% Quartile
68-73%	1	
< 68%	0	Below 25% Quartile

Future Analysis, Benchmarking, Insights and Assumptions:
(we continue to research and develop additional data points, trends and benchmarks)

Business Strategy Archetype: Strongest archetype tends to be - Customized Solutions Provider. This archetype tends to have strong internal programs on customer retention and return shoppers via strong promotions and marketing.

Industries to Watch: Manufacturing businesses tend to be quite strong in customer retention - many times due to the complexity and cost of switching suppliers.

Relevance of Company Size: No relevant significance found for retention due to a firm's size.

Exhibit 13-7

	Input	Incremental
Lead	Process	Distinctive
Lag	Result	Breakthrough

Metric Name: New Customers

IVS Category: Customer

Lead	Result	Distinctive

Definition: % of new customers that have bought products or services during the period.

Innovation Significance: New Customers buying your value proposition means that you are creating new, relevant value in the market and/or are finding new customers within the market.

Inputs & Formula:

	Units
New Customers per period / All Customers for period	%

Comments
New customers gives you a gauge on if your business is growing via new products, markets or more market penetration and if that growth is more than offsetting any loss of customers.

Related Metrics: Customer Penetration; Revenue Growth

APQC or General Best Practice Benchmarks

IVS Score Normalization:

%	Score
25%	10
23%	9
19%	8
16%	7
13%	6
10%	5
7%	4
4%	3
2%	2
1%	1
0%	0

Anything below 4% and you are not covering an average inflation rate

Future Analysis, Benchmarking, Insights and Assumptions:
(we continue to research and develop additional data points, trends and benchmarks)

Business Strategy Archetype: Strongest archetype tends to be - Customized Solutions Provider. This archetype lends itself to always be looking for new customers and finding new ways to please those customers.

Industries to Watch: Retail clients tend to have the most sophisticated programs focused on attracting new customers via promotions and incentives.

Relevance of Company Size: Larger businesses tend to be able to attract more new customers due to resource availiablity for marketing and business development campaigns along with their existing brand recognition.

Exhibit 13-8

		Input	Incremental
	Lead	Process	Distinctive
	Lag	Result	Breakthrough

Metric Name:	External Ideas			
IVS Category:	Customer	Lead	Process	Distinctive

Definition: Percent of innovation ideas that come into your business entity via outside constituents (customers, suppliers, agencies, consultants, universities, etc.) versus internal ideation.

Innovation Significance: A comprehensive pipeline of ideas is critical, and while internal ideas are great, especially for incremental and process ideas, research has found that external ideas can generate more distinctive and breakthrough ideas with higher associated outcomes and results versus process improvements.

	Units	**Comments**
Inputs & Formula: The number of innovation ideas sourced from outside the business entity, divided by the business entity's total number of innovation ideas, multiplied by 100%	%	As you implement ideation channels, be considerate of how to simply but accurately track the total number of ideas generated and submitted via all channels individually.

Related Metrics: Customer Engagement, Customer Satisfaction, Net Promoter Score, Strategic Accounts

APQC.

APQC or General Best Practice Benchmarks

IVS Score Normalization:		
60+%	10	Top 10% of Companies
50-59%	9	
40-49%	8	75% Quartile
35-39%	7	
30-34%	6	
20-29%	5	50% Quartile
18-19%	4	
16-17%	3	
14-15%	2	25% Quartile
12-13%	1	
< 12%	0	Below 25% Quartile

Future Analysis, Benchmarking, Insights and Assumptions:
(we continue to research and develop additional data points, trends and benchmarks)

Business Strategy Archetype: Strongest archetype tends to be - Customized Solutions Provider. Businesses that focus on customized customer solutions, by definition focus on external ideation as core to their value proposition.

Industries to Watch: Business Services organizations tend to be very attune to customer needs and seek the input of customers and market experts as they craft specific customer and market vertical offerings.

Relevance of Company Size: Small firms tend to be better at getting ideas from outside the firm. Larger companies tend to get inwardly focused, but have deep resources to use, while smaller firms go outside based on necessity.

Exhibit 13-9

		Input	Incremental
	Lead	Process	Distinctive
	Lag	Result	Breakthrough

Metric Name: Strategic Accounts

IVS Category: Customer

Lead	Result	Distinctive

Definition: The number of customer accounts you would classify as "strategic", or highly important to your organization.

Innovation Significance: Business management suggests that focusing in on strategic accounts aids in developing a value proposition that creates great value and demand. Those strategic accounts are key customers that generate business, generate ideas and are highly visible references and promoters of your business.

Inputs & Formula:

Units		Comments
Direct input metric. Subjective metric such that you track and monitor strategic accounts that you manage.	%	Companies delineate "strategic" accounts as those that they are willing to provide higher standards, lower prices, increased warranties, etc. from normal client accounts.

Related Metrics: Net Promoter Score; Customer Loyalty

APQC or General Best Practice Benchmarks

IVS Score Normalization:

20+%	10
17%	9
14%	8
11%	7
10%	6
7%	5
4%	4
1%	3
0%	2
0%	1
0%	0

Business best practice is that 20% of your business should be classified as "strategic accounts" and the other 80% are regular business accounts.

Future Analysis, Benchmarking, Insights and Assumptions:
(we continue to research and develop additional data points, trends and benchmarks)

Business Strategy Archetype: Strongest archetype tends to be - Customized Solutions Provider. These businesses tend to have strong client relationship managmenet teams which are skilled to segmented strategic accounts from normal accounts.

Industries to Watch: Business Services organizations due to their focus on industry verticals and customer specific needs tend to also be very good at segmenting strategic accounts and having special strategic account programs in place as part of their overall offerings.

Relevance of Company Size: Larger firms tend to be stronger at delineating customer accounts as a whole and offering different levels of service and expereince based on an account being a regular account or a "strategic" account.

Exhibit 13-10

			Input	Incremental
INNOVATION VALUE SCORE™		Lead Lag	Process Result	Distinctive Breakthrough
Metric Name:	CRM Strength			
IVS Category:	Customer	Lead	Process	Distinctive

Definition: CRM Strength is "promised" in many ways via utilizing CRM systems and methodologies and unfortunately measured in number of different ways as well. If your firm has a strong bias towards an effective CRM process, you likely measure this "strength" or effectiveness already.

Innovation Significance: CRM Strength means you are managing your customer relationships via retaining customers and delivering value to them such that they continue to buy from you. This is another key area of measurement for a company with a customer solutions/customer centric archetype strategy.

Inputs & Formula:

	Units	Comments
Direct input of a subjective self assessment grade	Letter Grade	CRM Strength can be measuring by several metrics in Sales, Marketing and Services related to a customer. CRM systems track many of these metrics. For IVS, this is a subjective self-assessed grade but should be based on your CRM metrics.

Related Metrics: Customer Satisfaction, Customer Retention, Customer Loyalty, Upsell, Cross Sell, Service Time, OTD, Close rate, Renewal rate, etc.

APQC or General Best Practice Benchmarks

IVS Score Normalization:

A+%	10
A	9
A-	8
na	7
B+	6
B	5
B-	4
C+	3
C	2
C-	1
less than a C-	0

No current benchmarks for this self-assessed metric.

Future Analysis, Benchmarking, Insights and Assumptions:
(we continue to research and develop additional data points, trends and benchmarks)

Business Strategy Archetype: Strongest archetype tends to be - Customized Solutions Provider. These businesses tend to have solid CRM systems in place to manage customers holistically and methodically across the organization.

Industries to Watch: Leading Technology businesses tend to be good at showcasing the use of technology and using technology to drive value - hence tech companies tend to be thoughtful and successful in the use of CRM systems.

Relevance of Company Size: Small firms tend not to be able to afford robust CRM systems or need a system to manage customer contacts and programs as a smaller team can more easily gather and review acounts manually. Large firms need these systems.

Exhibit 13-11

			Input	Incremental
		Lead	**Process**	**Distinctive**
		Lag	**Result**	**Breakthrough**

Metric Name: New Products

| **IVS Category:** | Growth | | **Lead** | **Result** | **Distinctive** |

Definition: The number of new product/service development projects currently in the design/build or manufacture/deliver stage of the product development function.

Innovation Significance: If you are a Product Developer archetype firm, this metric is especially critical. Are you executing and delivering new products to market that are relevant, timely and in a consistent fashion?

Inputs & Formula:

	Units	Comments
The number of new product/service development projects currently in the design/build or manufacture/deliver stage of the product development function.	%	This number reports the number of new product/service projects that are currently active in either the design/build or manufacture/deliver stage of the product development function.

Related Metrics: New IP, New Markets, New Customers

APQC.

APQC or General Best Practice Benchmarks

IVS Score Normalization:			
84+	10	Top 10% of Companies
59-83	9	
34-58	8	75% Quartile
24-33	7	
17-23	6	
12-16	5	50% Quartile
8-11	4	
7	3	
6	2	25% Quartile
5	1	
< 4	0	Below 25% Quartile

Future Analysis, Benchmarking, Insights and Assumptions:
(we continue to research and develop additional data points, trends and benchmarks)

Business Strategy Archetype:	Strongest archetype tends to be - Product Developer This archetype focuses on bringing multiple products to market and in an excellerated timeframe.
Industries to Watch:	Retail businesses tend to have short lifecycles of products and tend to churn (retire) products that are not moving to maximize shelfspace and financial returns.
Relevance of Company Size:	Small and mid sized companies have an advantage with new product development - they have less to risk and less bueracracy. Larger firms usually are less risk tolerant when they have a larger corporation to maintain and protect.

Exhibit 13-12

		Lead Lag	Input Process Result	Incremental Distinctive Breakthrough
Metric Name:	New Markets			
IVS Category:	Growth	Lead	Result	Breakthrough

Definition:
New Markets that your business is now actively selling into. New Markets can be more involved than adding new products and therefore are listed as breakthrough vs distinctive.

Innovation Significance:
Similar to New Products, New Markets is a critical metric for a Product Developer archetype firm. Are you delivering your products/services to new markets where you have little to no penetration?

Inputs & Formula:

	Units	Comments
# of New Markets entered into in the last 36 months / # of total markets currently served	%	Using the same definition as product, a market is no longer considered "new" after a 36 month window.

Related Metrics:
New IP, New Products, New Customers

APQC or General Best Practice Benchmarks

IVS Score Normalization:

60+%	10	
60%	9	
50%	8	
40%	7	
30%	6	Big Bang Disruption says you have to now reinvent yourself
20%	5	about every 5 years - new markets can be key to evolution.
10%	4	
5%	3	
4%	2	
2%	1	
0%	0	

Future Analysis, Benchmarking, Insights and Assumptions:
(we continue to research and develop additional data points, trends and benchmarks)

Business Strategy Archetype:
Strongest archetype tends to be - Product Developer
This archetype focuses on bringing products to tangiential or new markets from what they normally have served.

Industries to Watch:
Where as Retailers are strong at new products, Business Services tend to be better at new markets. Business Services organization tend to go to market within very specific market verticals, then extrapolate their offerings to new market verticals.

Relevance of Company Size:
Mid to large sized companies usually are better at penetrating new markets because they have a track record of success in one market that they can then parlay into a new market and have referencability.

Exhibit 13-13

		Input	Incremental
	Lead	**Process**	**Distinctive**
	Lag	**Result**	**Breakthrough**

Metric Name: | New IP

IVS Category: | Growth

Lead	Process	Breakthrough

Definition: New intellectual property added to the business via new patents, licenses, or trademarks granted through a regulatory or governing agency.

Innovation Significance: New IP via patents, licenses, etc., is normally a key metric in innovation, but it can not be the sole metric. Additionally, new IP that is created but not monetized produces little value. So while volume of development and a spirit of experimentation is fundamental, you need to be able to assess which ideas to patent, protect and trademark based on the value they can potentially create.

Inputs & Formula:

Inputs	Units	Comments
# of New Patents, Licenses, Trademarks in the last 36 months / total active patents, licenses, trademarks in company	%	Patents, licenses and trademarks are all very different levels of IP in a company - but all require investment and approval to obtain which can be a leading indicator to value creation.

Related Metrics: New Products, New Markets, New Customers, Customer Satisfaction, Customer Loyalty, Customer Cross-Sell

APQC or General Best Practice Benchmarks

IVS Score Normalization:

%	Score	
60+%	10	
60%	9	
50%	8	
40%	7	
30%	6	Big Bang Disruption says you have to now reinvent yourself
20%	5	about every 5 years
10%	4	
5%	3	
4%	2	
2%	1	
0%	0	

Future Analysis, Benchmarking, Insights and Assumptions:
(we continue to research and develop additional data points, trends and benchmarks)

Business Strategy Archetype: Strongest archetype tends to be - Product Developer This archetype holds IP in high regard and have internal processes to capture and protect IP through various stages of development.

Industries to Watch: Manufacuturing businesses tend to have some of the strongest mindsets towards IP and focus on patentability of products, processes and methods.

Relevance of Company Size: Similar to new products - small and mid sized companies have an advantage with new product development - they have less to risk, less bueracracy and more risk tolerant. Larger firms usually are less risk tolerant when they have a larger corporation to maintain and protect.

Exhibit 13-14

		Input	Incremental
	Lead	Process	Distinctive
	Lag	Result	Breakthrough

INNOVATION
VALUE SCORE

Metric Name:	Innovation Pipeline			

IVS Category:	Growth		Lead	Process	Distinctive

Definition: This is a cumulative point in time metric to measure the completeness of an innovation pipeline in a reporting period for a firm.

Innovation Significance: Balance in an innovation pipeline is key - not necessarily "equal" balance in all categories, but having a minimum of ideas in all categories and an imbalance in the categories most important to your firm.

		Units	**Comments**
Inputs & Formula:	Direct entry of metric based on summation of projects.	#	See rules below for how to score points

Related Metrics:	New Products, New Markets, Customer Satisfaction

APQC or General Best Practice Benchmarks

IVS Score Normalization:	na	10	Minimum of # concepts in each bucket of 50 Incremental, 25 Distinctive, 10 Breakthrough
	na	9	
	na	8	
	na	7	Company delineates projects between Incremental, Distinctive and Breakthrough and has entries in each category.
	na	6	
	na	5	
	na	4	Basic pipeline that counts # of ideas/concepts generated
	na	3	
	na	2	
	na	1	
	na	0	No tracking pipeline in place

Future Analysis, Benchmarking, Insights and Assumptions:
(we continue to research and develop additional data points, trends and benchmarks)

Business Strategy Archetype:	Strongest archetype tends to be - Product Developer These businesses normally have strong, robust stage gate processes in place, as well as capital processes that have a strong bent towards new investment.

Industries to Watch:	Technology firms - in particular Biotech and Software firms are normally very adept at planning releases, upgrades and enhancements to existing products to extend products and services and that materializes from having a strong release pipeline of projects in play.

Relevance of Company Size:	Larger companies tend to be more focused on having an overall portfolio of products and services and have the resources to develop and implement multiple things simultaneously versus small firms that may be more limited with resources and also in business maturity.

Exhibit 13-15

		Input	Incremental
	Lead	**Process**	**Distinctive**
	Lag	**Result**	**Breakthrough**

INNOVATION VALUE SCORE

Metric Name:	Brand Awareness			
IVS Category:	Growth	Lead	Input	Distinctive

Definition: Percentage of customers who can name brand in an unaided recall test

Innovation Significance: Growth comes through market adoption and interest. Market adoption and interest comes from potential customers "seeing" you and your products. Therefore, the volume AND effectiveness of these impressions are critical.

	Units	*Comments*
Inputs & Formula: The number of customers who can name brand in unaided recall test, divided by the total number of customers who participated in unaided recall test, multiplied by 100%	%	Companies run various campaigns to elevate and broaden the recognition of their company brand and logo. Marketing tends to measure this on a reoccurring basis and also specifically to new initiatives to measure brand lift and interest by the market.

Related Metrics: Reputation, Net Promoter Score

APQC.

APQC or General Best Practice Benchmarks

IVS Score Normalization:		
90+%	10	Top 10% of Companies
87-89%	9	
85-87%	8	75% Quartile
82-85%	7	
74-81%	6	
70-75%	5	50% Quartile
65-69%	4	
55-64%	3	
46-54%	2	25% Quartile
37-46%	1	
<37%	0	Below 25% Quartile

Future Analysis, Benchmarking, Insights and Assumptions:
(we continue to research and develop additional data points, trends and benchmarks)

Business Strategy Archetype: Strongest archetype tends to be - Product Developer
This archetype builds a strong consumer brand and focuses on similar products that their customer base would expect from them to drive more sales.

Industries to Watch: Retail companies are focused, and some are obsessed with Brand awareness. They tend to dedicate the most resources among companies to brand and have the most focus on its impact.

Relevance of Company Size: Larger companies, unless you have a very disruptive brand and campaign, normally achieve greater results through their massive marketing budgets and multiple-pronged approaches to build brand awareness with multiple offerings.

Exhibit 13-16

		Input	Incremental
	Lead	Process	Distinctive
	Lag	Result	Breakthrough

INNOVATION VALUE SCORE

Metric Name:	Speed to Market			
IVS Category:	Growth	Lead	Process	Distinctive

Definition: Time-to-market reports the average cycle time from the design/build phase to the manufacture/deliver stage until the product release for new products/services.

Innovation Significance: Speed to market is critical, especially for a Product Developer archetype strategy business. If you bring good products/services to market, but it takes you a long time you may lose first mover advantages, premium pricing and market share.

		Units	Comments
Inputs & Formula:	Direct Input metric. The average cycle time from the design/build phase to the manufacture/deliver stage until the product release for new products/services.	# days	In your project management, budgeting and capital management disciplines, ensure that you are tracking idea timelines from initial conception to when you actually deliver a product/service to market.

Related Metrics: New Products, Customer Satisfaction

APQC.

APQC or General Best Practice Benchmarks

IVS Score Normalization:			
132 or < days	10	Top 10% of Companies
133-150	9	
151-175	8	75% Quartile
176-209	7	
210-249	6	
250-275	5	50% Quartile
276-325	4	
326-375	3	
376-425	2	25% Quartile
426-450	1	
> 450	0	Below 25% Quartile

Future Analysis, Benchmarking, Insights and Assumptions:
(we continue to research and develop additional data points, trends and benchmarks)

Business Strategy Archetype:	Strongest archetype tends to be - Product Developer This archetype focuses on bringing products to market in an excellerated timeframe to meet some new or potential market trend.
Industries to Watch:	Retail organizations again tend to dominate speed to market with new products being plentiful and shelf/floor space being limited - they introduce new products and bring them to market quickly based on customer buying patterns and trending.
Relevance of Company Size:	Smaller companies tend to be much faster at getting to market with new products as they don't have the "burden" of infrastructure and multiple levels of approvals and controls that you'll find in larger firms.

Exhibit 13-17

		Input	Incremental
	Lead	Process	Distinctive
	Lag	Result	Breakthrough

Metric Name: On Time Delivery (OTD)

IVS Category: Operations/People

Lag	Process	Incremental

Definition: Orders that are shipped on time to the original customer promised delivery date.

Innovation Significance: If you are not delivering on today's value proposition, today's customer's will go to your competitors for tomorrow's new products or simply replace you today.

Inputs & Formula:

	Units	*Comments*
# of orders shipped to delivery date / # of total orders	%	OTD metrics can be manipulated to increase scores by adjusting promise dates to new/revised promise dates. Best practice measurement of this metric uses the original promise date for the best measurement and establishing a high level of excellence.

Related Metrics: Customer Satisfaction, Customer Loyalty, Customer Retention, Net Promoter

APQC or General Best Practice Benchmarks

IVS Score Normalization:

99+%	10	
95%	9	
90%	8	
85%	7	
80%	6	
75%	5	Best practice levels at high execution level companies.
70%	4	
60%	3	
65%	2	
50%	1	
less than 50%	0	

Future Analysis, Benchmarking, Insights and Assumptions:
(we continue to research and develop additional data points, trends and benchmarks)

Business Strategy Archetype: Strongest archetype tends to be - Best Price/Low Cost Leader. These firms are keenly focused on delivery - and they have strong manufacturing and operational processes to deliver products on time to customers.

Industries to Watch: Manufacturing firms in general have the strongest propensity to manage to OTD deadlines from customers, many times because they are a compoentnt in a larger solution and timelines have been specifically negotiated and agreed upon.

Relevance of Company Size: Size does not have a significant relevance in OTD. Smaller firms are anxious to deliver for new and fewer clients and are able to drive execution to completion; larger firms have stronger processes and tend to be more tight in operations leading to solid OTD rates as well.

Exhibit 13-18

		Lead Lag	Input Process Result	Incremental Distinctive Breakthrough
Metric Name:	Employee Retention			
IVS Category:	Operations/People	Lead	Input	Incremental

Definition: Gross number of employees that continue working in your business over a period of time.

Innovation Significance: Employees are key to your business and delivering on your value proposition - they are the "inputs" which take other resources and turn them into value for your customers.

Inputs & Formula:	# of employees employed at end of period (less new adds) / # of total employees at beginning of period	Units %	Comments
			Voluntary and involuntary turnover are sometimes discluded to show a more accurate level of retention, we advise leaving turnover numbers as part of this metric. Voluntary turnover may lead to an issue around culture and environment, and involuntary to improper resource management - either represents employee churn in the business.

Related Metrics: Employee Satisfaction; Employee Engagement; Employee Turnover; Culture Index

APQC

APQC or General Best Practice Benchmarks

IVS Score Normalization:		
98+%	10	Top 10% of Companies
96-97%	9	
94-95%	8	75% Quartile
92-93%	7	
91-92%	6	
89-90%	5	50% Quartile
87-88%	4	
85-86%	3	
83-84%	2	25% Quartile
81-83%	1	
<81%	0	Below 25% Quartile

Future Analysis, Benchmarking, Insights and Assumptions:
(we continue to research and develop additional data points, trends and benchmarks)

Business Strategy Archetype:	Strongest archetype tends to be - Best Price/Low Cost Leader. These businesses tend to me more mature, more stable and they know the profile and skillset of the employees they want to hire - and when hiring is done well, retention many times follows.
Industries to Watch:	Institutions tend to have very high employee retention rates and employee longetivity.
Relevance of Company Size:	We believe mid sized firms have some of the best retention and engagement simply because you are inbetween being resource contrainted as many smaller firms are, and overly structured as larger firms tend to be - providing an overall comfortable fit for employees.

Exhibit 13-19

	Lead	Input Process Lag	Incremental Distinctive Breakthrough

Metric Name:	Employee Engagement		
IVS Category:	Operations/People	Lead	Input	Distinctive

Definition: This metric is normally calculated by an external agency which does an annual "employee engagement survey". Employee engagement in the business is measured by a number of qualitative questions to all employees which then assesses how committed or "engaged" an employee is in the company's welfare.

Innovation Significance: Similar to retention and even more germane here, employees are the "inputs" which take other resources and turn them into value for your customers. Especially if your business archetype is Best Price/Low Cost Leader, a highly engaged workforce is critical for executional success.

Inputs & Formula:		Units	**Comments**
	Direct Input - Survey Result	%	Employee engagement is normally measured by a third party on an annual basis to determine "engagement" of employees in the business. Surveys are normally compared year over year for trending purposes and to monitor improvements or declines.

Related Metrics:	Employee Satisfaction; Employee Engagement; Employee Turnover; Culture Index

APQC or General Best Practice Benchmarks

IVS Score Normalization:		
	99+%	10
	95%	9
	93%	8
	90%	7
	85%	6
	80%	5
	75%	4
	70%	3
	65%	2
	60%	1
	55%	0

Benchmarks partially extrapolated from employee retention and other benchmarks.

Future Analysis, Benchmarking, Insights and Assumptions:
(we continue to research and develop additional data points, trends and benchmarks)

Business Strategy Archetype: Strongest archetype tends to be - Best Price/Low Cost Leader. Similar to rentention, a stable workforce tends to lead to higher levels of satisfaction and engagement.

Industries to Watch: Healthcare firms tend to have higher employee engagement than most industries as many healthcare employees are in that industry due to a personal mission or personal expereince.

Relevance of Company Size: We believe mid sized firms have some of the best retention and engagement simply because you are inbetween being resource contrainted as many smaller firms are, and overly structured as larger firms tend to be.

Exhibit 13-20

INNOVATION
VALUE SCORE

		Lead Lag	Input Process Result	Incremental Distinctive Breakthrough
Metric Name:	Training Dollars			
IVS Category:	Operations/People	Lead	Input	Incremental

Definition: Training dollars reported in total for all employees via internal and external training sessions attended.

Innovation Significance: If employees are key inputs in turning other resources into value, the better informed and trained those employees are, the better value they can create. If your business archetype is Best Price/Low Cost Leader, operational excellence is more readily achieved with a knowledgeable workforce.

Inputs & Formula:

	Units	Comments
Total cost to "develop and counsel employees," divided by the number of business entity employees.	$	Training investments include training programs and costs associated with orientation, performance improvement, development and overall training via both internal and externally provided programs.

Related Metrics: Productivity; Knowledge Management, Employee Engagement

APQC.

APQC or General Best Practice Benchmarks

IVS Score Normalization:

$600	10	Top 10% of Companies
$520-599	9	
$475-519	8	75% Quartile
$425-475	7	
$400-424	6	
$350-399	5	50% Quartile
$300-349	4	
$250-299	3	
$200-249	2	25% Quartile
$125-199	1	
< $125	0	Below 25% Quartile

Future Analysis, Benchmarking, Insights and Assumptions:
(we continue to research and develop additional data points, trends and benchmarks)

Business Strategy Archetype: Strongest archetype tends to be - Best Price/Low Cost Leader. Businesses focused on best price and lowest cost focus on reduction of variation. Variation reduction is achieved by consistency and training.

Industries to Watch: Technology firms tend to invest the most in employee development via bootcamps, advanced training, sales and product training. This training is also specilized for fewer people than you'd see in a manufacturing environment therefore with a higher cost of training per employee.

Relevance of Company Size: Mid sized firms tend to be best in many training areas as they don't require as large of budgets due to large company volume but yet they have more resources than smaller companies.

Exhibit 13-21

	Lead / Lag	Input Process Result	Incremental Distinctive Breakthrough

Metric Name: Quality - Returns

IVS Category: Operations/People | Lag | Process | Incremental

Definition: Quality can be measuring in numerous fashions including product returns and quality defects via processing. For this metric we are simply using sales returns by customers as a gauge of quality.

Innovation Significance: Customers will not repeatedly buy a low quality product. If your products have quality issues such that they are being returned, this is an area for potential innovation process improvement.

Inputs & Formula:

	Units	Comments
Value of returned orders/Value of total orders in period	%	Quality can be measuring in numerous fashions including product returns and quality defects via processing. We believe product returns to be one of the most universal quality metrics.

Related Metrics: Defects, Productivity; Training, Time to Market

APQC.

APQC or General Best Practice Benchmarks

IVS Score Normalization:

Benchmark	Score	Quartile
0.5 and <%	10	Top 10% of Companies
0.6%	9	
0.7%	8	75% Quartile
0.8%	7	
0.9%	6	
1.0%	5	50% Quartile
1.3%	4	
1.5%	3	
2.0%	2	25% Quartile
2.5%	1	
> 2.5%	0	Below 25% Quartile

Future Analysis, Benchmarking, Insights and Assumptions:
(we continue to research and develop additional data points, trends and benchmarks)

Business Strategy Archetype: Strongest archetype tends to be - Best Price/Low Cost Leader. Businesses focused on best price and lowest cost focus on reduction of variation. Variation reduction leads to higher levels of quality.

Industries to Watch: Manufacturing firms are most comfortable with Six Sigma, Lean and other operational improvement and quality processes and tend to be required to track lots and batches for quality control and recall issues.

Relevance of Company Size: Larger firms tend to be best at achieving high levels of quality as they are continuously focused on operations and execution at higher quantities so naturally they have a need to focus on quality to achieve volumes and customer comittments.

Exhibit 13-22

INNOVATION VALUE SCORE

	Lead Lag	Input Process Result	Incremental Distinctive Breakthrough

Metric Name: Supplier Value

IVS Category: Operations/People

Lag	Process	Incremental

Definition: The dollar value that a supplier contributes to your business either via cost savings, a reduction in their price to you or added value that you can charge more for, or revenue generating opportunities that they initiate that contributes to an increase in your sales.

Innovation Significance: Suppliers can be great providers of value - in what you outsource to them to provide to you and in ideas of how to deliver more value to the end customer. Many times engaging your suppliers in that second aspect can make them more of a business partner and drive more value.

Inputs & Formula:

	Units	Comments
(cost savings + new revenue sourced) / total supplier contract value	%	Suppliers that are strategic partners should be coming forward with initiatives in supply chain savings or new product enhancements (that generate revenue) they can support and provide to your business.

Related Metrics: Productivity; Efficiency; Product Extensions

APQC or General Best Practice Benchmarks

IVS Score Normalization:

%	Score
25+%	10
20%	9
15%	8
10%	7
5%	6
0%	5
-5%	4
-10%	3
-15%	2
-20%	1
-20+%	0

-5% would represents a supplier cost increase and no additional value creation and therefore land in the yellow zone. Other benchmarks interpolated from this beginning point.

Future Analysis, Benchmarking, Insights and Assumptions:
(we continue to research and develop additional data points, trends and benchmarks)

Business Strategy Archetype: Strongest archetype tends to be - Best Price/Low Cost Leader. Low variation and high quality can only be achieved by a strong supply chain. Therefore, these businesses tend to effectively manage suppliers and create win-win scenarios to maximize value.

Industries to Watch: Manufacturing firms tend to be some of the best companies at manging their supply chain and having suppliers that in turn create value that can transsend to their own value proposition.

Relevance of Company Size: Larger firms definitely have an advantage with soliciting and receiving supplier value. Similar to strategy accounts, suppliers can dedicate more time and resources to larger firms and work on projects to drive more value to them - or they risk losing a large customer.

Exhibit 13-23

			Input	Incremental
		Lead	Process	Distinctive
		Lag	Result	Breakthrough

INNOVATION VALUE SCORE					
Metric Name:	New Product Revenue				
IVS Category:	Financial		Lag	Result	Distinctive

Definition: Revenue generated from new products introduced during the past 12 months.

Innovation Significance: This metric moves beyond ideas submitted and introduced to the level of monetization of those new products and services. This should be a leading indicator to the health of your overall value proposition.

	Units	**Comments**
Inputs & Formula: Sales revenue from products/services launched in the past fiscal year, divided by the total sales revenue in the past fiscal year.	%	Industries may vary on how fast they need to replace their current value proposition, but aside from that chasm, it's advisable to measure this metric and determine the appropriate levels in your business and industry.

Related Metrics: Growth; # New Products, # New Markets

APQC

APQC or General Best Practice Benchmarks

IVS Score Normalization:			
40+%	10	Top 10% of Companies
30-39%	9	
20-29%	8	75% Quartile
17-19%	7	
15-17%	6	
13-14%	5	50% Quartile
11-12%	4	
9-10%	3	
7-8%	2	25% Quartile
6-7%	1	
< 6%	0	Below 25% Quartile

Future Analysis, Benchmarking, Insights and Assumptions:
(we continue to research and develop additional data points, trends and benchmarks)

Business Strategy Archetype:	Strongest archetype tends to be - Proprietary Leader. These businesses tend to have dominate market positions and while the revenue may all come from only one product or product line, it tends to be substantial.
Industries to Watch:	Retail companies tend to see larger rates of new product revenue, but they also have short product lifecycles and are continusouly changing out products for new and improved ones.
Relevance of Company Size:	Larger companies have more resources with which to bring new products to market, so many times should have higher rates of new product revenue than smaller firms, expect when a large firm's base is high to begin with, large absolute dollars in new revenue are a small percentage overall.

Exhibit 13-24

		Input	Incremental
	Lead	Process	Distinctive
	Lag	Result	Breakthrough

INNOVATION
VALUE SCORE

Metric Name:	Capital to Revenue			
IVS Category:	Financial	Lead	Input	Distinctive

Definition: Capital invested in a prior period compared to revenue in the current period

Innovation Significance: Capital investment is normally required to grow and sustain a healthy business. For a proprietary leader archetype business, capital investment and growth generated from that investment is paramount.

	Units	**Comments**
Inputs & Formula: Capitalized investment 24 months ago / current period revenue	%	This metric intends to capture the revenue generated from capital investments. This metric attempts to match the lag period capital, meaning the capital that was capitalized on the books from the prior 24 month period divided by the revenue from the current 24 month period.

Related Metrics: Growth; # New Products, # New Markets, ROIC

APQC or General Best Practice Benchmarks

IVS Score Normalization:

25+%	10
20%	9
17%	8
13%	7
10%	6
7%	5
5%	4
3%	3
1%	2
0%	1
na	0

Insuffient data currently available for this benchmark.

Future Analysis, Benchmarking, Insights and Assumptions:
(we continue to research and develop additional data points, trends and benchmarks)

Business Strategy Archetype: Strongest archetype tends to be - Proprietary Leader. These businesses have very specific and focused go to market plans and early mover status.

Industries to Watch: Disruptive manafacturing firms through the use of new technology, like 3D printing can be some of the most notable propritary leaders and have some of the highest capital returns due to initial pricing levels.

Relevance of Company Size: Larger firms tend to have more capital to deploy - the question is, do they spend it in the right areas for innovation value?

Exhibit 13-25

	Input	Incremental
Lead	Process	Distinctive
Lag	Result	Breakthrough

Metric Name: Gross Margin Improvement

IVS Category:	Financial		Lag	Process	Incremental

Definition: Current period gross margin (revenue less cost of goods sold) percent less prior period gross margin percent.

Innovation Significance: Gross margin improvements over time is critical to all types of businesses across their entire portfolio of products.

	Units	**Comments**
Inputs & Formula: Current period GM % minus prior period GM%	#	Gross margin is meant to evaluate cost improvements to products vs SG&A elements in net income %'s.

Related Metrics: Operational Efficiency, Net Income%

APQC or General Best Practice Benchmarks

IVS Score Normalization:		
1000 basis points	10	
750	9	
500	8	
250	7	
150	6	Insufficent data for full benchmarks, but several datapoints
100	5	used to calculate this spread.
50	4	
25	3	
10	2	
5	1	
0 or negative	0	

Future Analysis, Benchmarking, Insights and Assumptions:
(we continue to research and develop additional data points, trends and benchmarks)

Business Strategy Archetype: Strongest archetype tends to be - Proprietary Leader. These businesses normally have little competition and can charge premium price levels leading to high gross margins.

Industries to Watch: Both manufacturing and retail firms tend to lead in this area. Both types of companies are continously, quarter or quarter applying resources to find more and better ways to reduce COGS and improve overall GM levels.

Relevance of Company Size: Larger firms tend to have a large focus on improving GM levels due to the sheer value that it creates.

Exhibit 13-26

		Lead	Input	Incremental
		Lag	Process	Distinctive
			Result	Breakthrough

Metric Name:	Free Cash Flow			
IVS Category:	Financial	Lag	Result	Incremental

Definition: Free cash flow from the period divided by operating cash flow for the same period

Innovation Significance: In the financial category, it is important to monitor the amount of "real" cash that is being generated in the business to ensure you are monetizing the business and maximizing your assets and returns while you in a dominate market position - especially those businesses currently in a proprietary leader strategy position.

		Units	**Comments**
Inputs & Formula:	FCF/Operating Cash Flow	%	Free cash flow can indicate the "real" amount of cash that a company earns. Therefore, the ratio of free cash flow to operating cash flow measures of how much of a company's cash is produced and saved versus used for operations or reinvested.

Related Metrics: Various Cash Flow metrics

APQC or General Best Practice Benchmarks

IVS Score Normalization:		
	60+%	10
	50%	9
	40%	8
	35%	7
	30%	6
	25%	5
	20%	4
	10%	3
	5%	2
	0%	1
	na	0

Modeled after similar cash flow benchmarks.

Future Analysis, Benchmarking, Insights and Assumptions:
(we continue to research and develop additional data points, trends and benchmarks)

Business Strategy Archetype:	Strongest archetype tends to be - Proprietary Leader. These businesses in the early stage tend to generate significant cash flow from high pricing due to lack of competition. FCF falls off quickly with competition and price reductions.
Industries to Watch:	Business Services firms tend to have strong people resources and priorary methods and processes, but less in the form of capital invesment therefore leading to high FCF.
Relevance of Company Size:	Data points are inconclusive. Many small, med sized and large firms are good at managing cash flow, and an equal amount are bad at it. Cash flow management needs to be an important strategic focus and understood well at the executive level.

INNOVATION
VALUE SCORE

Exhibit 13-27

INNOVATION
VALUE SCORE

		Input	Incremental
	Lead	Process	Distinctive
	Lag	Result	Breakthrough

Metric Name:	Return on Assets			
IVS Category:	Financial	Lag	Result	Distinctive

Definition: Net income divided by total assets.

Innovation Significance: At some point, businesses need to consider a shedding of assets to ensure they preserve the results and returns they have generated to date. Therefore, in a Proprietary leader archetype, looking at income to assets is key to consider, discuss and evaluate exiting choices and timing scenarios.

Inputs & Formula:		Units	**Comments**
	Net Income / Total Assets	#	The ratio does not include any future commitments regarding assets, nor does it include the cost of replacing older ones.

Related Metrics: RONA

APQC.

APQC or General Best Practice Benchmarks

IVS Score Normalization:	118+%	10	Top 10% of Companies
	80-117%	9	
	38-79%	8	75% Quartile
	28-37%	7	
	18-27%	6	
	12-17%	5	50% Quartile
	9-11%	4	
	6-8%	3	
	4-5%	2	25% Quartile
	2-3%	1	
	<2%	0	Below 25% Quartile

Future Analysis, Benchmarking, Insights and Assumptions:
(we continue to research and develop additional data points, trends and benchmarks)

Business Strategy Archetype: Strategy archetype is less a factor in best examples of this metric as the best metrics come for those firms that are the least capital intensive and have fair to high returns such as Business Services companies.

Industries to Watch: Business Services firms that have little in the way of large, hard capital investment and where their investment is made up of people and processes tend to have highest ROA returns.

Relevance of Company Size: No significance found in size of company with this benchmark.

Exhibit 13-28

INNOVATION VALUE SCORE

		Input	Incremental
	Lead	Process	Distinctive
	Lag	Result	Breakthrough

Metric Name: Product & Market Exits

IVS Category: Financial

	Lag	Process	Distinctive

Definition: The number of products and or markets your businesses has exited from in the reporting period.

Innovation Significance: In a traditional "S curve" or product lifecycle, products/services eventually go through decline and if not reinvented, the firm needs to assess when to exit the market. This metric is meant to facilitate that consideration as a healthy firm will strategically exit products and markets as needed versus continuing to invest in a declining product or market.

Inputs & Formula:

	Units	Comments
# of products & markets exited/total products & markets	%	This is an inverse of the new product and market additions metrics - the strength in this metric is determining if the business is shedding weight and reinventing itself.

Related Metrics: # new products; # new markets, ROIC, RONA

APQC or General Best Practice Benchmarks

IVS Score Normalization:

30+%	10	
25%	9	
22.5%	8	
20%	7	Little research or data is available for this or similar metrics.
17.5%	6	If is far easier to determine when to get into a market and
15%	5	begin a product lifecycle compared to when to exit a market
10%	4	or sunset a product.
5%	3	
2.5%	2	
0%	1	
na	0	

Future Analysis, Benchmarking, Insights and Assumptions:
(we continue to research and develop additional data points, trends and benchmarks)

Business Strategy Archetype: We have not captured or expereinced enough datapoints or cases for this metric to yet draw a conclusion on best strategy archetype.

Industries to Watch: There are few companies overall that are good at knowing when/where to exit markets, much less entire industries. No significance is currently found in industries that are better than others.

Relevance of Company Size: Mid sized firms are likely the best in this area. Smaller firms need to continue to drive in markets probably longer than they should because they may not have other markets to go to, and large firms tend not to be good at exiting anything and products take on lives of their own unless someone steps up to exit from a market.

**Exhibit 13-29: Respondents' Opinions about
the Usefulness of the IVS Approach**

Question: *In your opinion, do you think the following aspects of the
IVS approach would be helpful to your organization?*

	Not helpful (%)	Somewhat helpful (%)	Very helpful (%)	Extremely Helpful (%)
BSC framework	3	29	52	16
Breakdowns by incremental, distinctive, and breakthrough	3	45	36	16
Breakdowns by leading and lagging indicators	6	36	32	26
Reporting comparisons and actionability	6	22	36	36

Measuring, monitoring, and improving these 24 metrics—and managing them according to your business strategy—will improve your overall innovation value creation and the value proposition that you put forward to your customers and to the market.

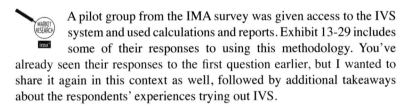 A pilot group from the IMA survey was given access to the IVS system and used calculations and reports. Exhibit 13-29 includes some of their responses to using this methodology. You've already seen their responses to the first question earlier, but I wanted to share it again in this context as well, followed by additional takeaways about the respondents' experiences trying out IVS.

- Using an existing framework like a BSC can be *very/extremely Helpful.*

- Having some different cuts (incremental/distinctive/breakthrough and leading and lagging) to compare, contrast, debate, and discuss results is *somewhat/very helpful.*

- Above all, 72% like actionability and comparability in reporting. They want to measure these indicators, but they ultimately want to determine the steps of improvement to drive more value and have the ability to compare and contrast results with other businesses.

Four other key takeaways from this pilot review:

- *Usability is key, like any other system.* While 67% said IVS was *easy* or *fairly easy* to use, 33% said it was *difficult*. This shows an opportunity to continue to improve the system and make sure people know how to use it and extract value expediently.

- *Data may or may not be readily available.* Here, 62% said that estimating and consolidating data for entry into IVS was *easy* or *fairly easy*. But the remaining 38% said it was somewhat *difficult*. One point of consideration in choosing the IVS metrics was data availability. Similar to your first scorecarding experience, many people don't always track the data for the metrics they would like to be looking at, and it can take some work to put tracking mechanisms in place. Although this pain is understandable, go back to the mantra of *"If you can't measure it, you can't improve it."* You may not need to track all 24 IVS metrics, but you should focus on tracking or (at least) estimating the most important ones for your business.

- *These metrics resonate.* 57% said the IVS metrics would be *very helpful* to their organization in measuring, reporting on, and making improvements to innovation and value creation. Another 20% said they would be *moderately helpful*, 7% said they would be *extremely helpful*, and 0% saying they would *not be helpful*.

- *Some metric surprises.* Respondents were asked which metrics specifically would provide the *least* value for innovation measurement. It was slightly surprising that the top three vote-getters here were:
  - 36%: New IP
  - 29%: External Ideas
  - 19%: Return on Assets

As discussed in the Introduction to Part III, many people associate innovation with technology, which can correspond to patents and licenses around that technology. I was happy to see that this was not one of the most important singular metrics, but I still believe it is an appropriate metric for many of us to keep an eye on in innovation value creation.

There is a bit more concern about the 29% who said they didn't value ideas that came from outside their business. I believe that best-in-class companies get about 50% of their ideas from outside their company, which is confirmed by the APQC benchmark.

FOUR BUSINESS ARCHETYPES

As mentioned in Chapter 12, there are no "weightings" in the IVS calculations, and there isn't one metric that everyone should view as greater than other metrics. The reason for this lies in the differences in business strategy. Some businesses require different results and have different roles because of their strategy. So while a balanced approach and using a BSC format to measure innovation value is logical, you have to interpret where you should have imbalance and which metrics are more important to your specific business. That is where the concept of business archetypes comes into play.

Now that you have a feel for the metrics that go into calculating your individual category IVS scores and associated composite scores, let's talk about your expectations around the results and then get into the reporting and recommendations for taking action.

> **Comparing your metrics to a company that has a similar strategic archetype is critical and most meaningful.**

When Kaplan and Norton came out with the BSC in the early 1990s, they followed that initial work with research, observations, and recommendations around the need to have strategy maps. If you talk with them directly, or simply read their books, they would tell you that the *Strategy Maps* and *The Strategy Focused Organization* books really should have come out before *The Balanced Scorecard*. Why? Because you get what you measure. And a BSC of metrics (not all of which are financial) is superior thinking and advice, but you can still be measuring the wrong things.

Therefore, it is *critical* that you have your strategy articulated and tied to specific metrics and initiatives. *Then* you will be measuring what is important and what you are strategically striving toward. Consider the definition of value proposition:

> *"The value proposition defines the company's strategy for the customer by describing the unique mix of product, price, service, relationship and image that a company offers its targeted group of customers. The value proposition should communicate what the company expects to do for its customer* **better** *or* differently *than its competitors."*[26]

There are four business archetypes of value propositions:

1. *Low/Best Price Leader*—low-cost, high-quality, fast. These firms create processes designed to produce results consistently, with low

variability and speed. Examples are Walmart, Southwest Airlines, and McDonald's.

2. ***Product Developer***—high-performance products, first-to-market positioning and in penetrating new markets. These firms have a shorter time to market than most, quick trials, and tend to launch more products and get into multiple markets. Examples include Apple, Sony, and Intel.

3. ***Customized Solutions Provider***—Provide customized products and services tailored to each customer. Examples include IBM and Goldman Sachs.

4. ***Proprietary Leader***—when companies create a propriety product, platform, or system based on revolutionary leadership or deep business insight and creativity. A "monopoly" or market dominating position would be an overstated description, but it paints a vivid picture of which firms fall into this category. Examples are eBay and Google.

Why is this discussion of different value propositions and archetypes important? Because you should expect to see differing IVS scores and summaries depending on your business and your archetype. APQC's open innovation research found similar archetypes and discussed the important aspect that *"because there is no single model of innovation that works for all firms, companies get into trouble by trying to imitate a company that is very much* unlike *them."*[27] You can't simply say, "We should have the highest scores in all IVS categories and measures." That doesn't make sense. You have a strategic focus and should have an imbalance that matches your priorities, but you shouldn't ignore other categories outright. Therefore, you should have an imbalanced IVS score that has high results in the category that aligns to your strategy archetype, and you should expect moderate or maybe even lower results in some of the other areas. But don't dismiss metrics or categories completely. For example:

- If you are a Low/Best Price Leader company, then you should expect to have high IVS metric scores in the financial category and lower IVS metric scores in the growth category because you are focused on having few offerings and providing your products very efficiently.

- If you are a Product Developer company, you should expect to have high IVS metric scores in the growth category and likely lower IVS scores in the operations and financial categories to a degree because you are focused on new products and not necessarily the scale of operations, at least initially.

These archetypes set your expectations for your IVS scores as well as what you should take action on and the anticipated, expected, and desired results. While you'd conceptually like to see high scores in every category, that may not make sense strategically with your business and its current value proposition and positioning. You may allow some lower scores on financial metrics and efficiency to achieve higher product leadership results. You may be in a harvesting and exiting mode and need to drive efficiencies and financial metrics to the detriment of investment and growth areas.

The point is: Your IVS scores need to match your business's strategy and have some level of balance, and that balance and where it is disproportionate depends on your strategy. This is also why there are no weightings by category or individual metrics—the categories and metrics have differing levels of importance for different companies depending on their strategies. Businesses should keep an eye on all metrics and strive for some minimal levels in some areas while focusing their highest achievement, time, and attention on the metrics that align to their strategy. The next sections of this chapter show a mapping of strategic archetypes to IVS categories.

Archetype #1: Low/Best Price Leader

Companies in this category should have the highest IVS scores in the operational excellence category. They tend to spend more time on incremental and distinctive innovations to their value proposition than on breakthroughs, with a focus on process improvements vs. volume of inputs. They are in a growth or early harvest business phase and are trying to maximize the returns on their investments.

Archetype #2: Product Developer

Companies in this category should have the highest IVS scores in growth and advancement. These firms tend to spend a disproportionate amount of time on advancing new products and working on new markets. They are expected to ideate and experiment quickly and are comfortable doing so. When they govern their innovation process, they focus on inputs and getting a large volume of inputs to find a smaller number of winning ideas that they can make money on as the first mover in the market.

Archetype #3: Customized Solutions Provider

Companies in this category should have the highest IVS scores in customer value. These firms are very customer-centric; you see it in their values, you hear it in the way they talk, and you should hear it from their customers, who are raving fans.

They should also have solid scores in growth and advancement since that is the leading indicator channel in which these companies can create more value in the future for the customer value category. These firms tend to—not always, but tend to—focus in a secondary fashion on operational excellence and financial.

Archetype #4: Proprietary Leader

This category isn't matched as easily as the others, but it is still relevant. These firms likely have the strongest IVS scores in the financial category. If they are an early leader, a pioneer of a new system, platform, product, and so on, they focus on how fast they can scale their offering and maintain a dominate position. They require balance via some of the other categories, but many times firms in this archetype come down to basic financial metrics and how they are maximizing returns as much as possible during their time of proprietary leadership and dominance.

Two key metrics that are more significant than many of the other IVS metrics to these firms are Product & Market Exits and Return on Assets. At some point, firms in this archetype need to look at when and how to shed assets and maintain the financial returns generated vs. investing in a value proposition that is in decline.

Exhibit 13-30 maps each archetype to each of the IVS categories and what you should expect to find based on your archetype. Note the "Watch" areas, as they are natural areas that can be overlooked due to the business strategy you have in play, and they can create issues if not monitored.

BUSINESS ARCHETYPES—IVS EXPECTED RESULTS

Comparability—Value vs. Noise

After you select your metrics in IVS and enter your data, you get your IVS calculations and results. After you get your IVS results, you need to apply judgement and experience to use this information. I suggest starting with the principles discussed in the following sections.

The Overall IVS Score

The overall IVS score is good to *begin* a conversation and to show some comparability between business units and divisions within a company in order to establish a general understanding about positioning and innovation value creation. There is also some value in looking at the total IVS score in relation to other firms with similar demographics, such as the

Exhibit 13-30

IVS *Expectations* by Archetype

IVS Categories	Business Strategy Archetypes			
	Customized Solutions Provider	**Low/Best Price Leader**	**Product Developer**	**Proprietary Leader**
Customer Value	**Highest IVS** Businesses are very customer centric and should score high in these metrics.	**Watch** Retention and satisfaction are key, but can become too inwardly focused.	**Medium** Looking for new customers, but more focus on strong CRM and keeping and serving strategic accounts.	**Medium** Standard customer care, but little over the top or special programs.
Growth & Advancement	**Medium** Experimenting with new products/markets that you think will be receptive with some customization.	**Lower** More of a fast follower than an inventor by design.	**Highest IVS** Constantly pushing boundaries and looking for next new thing.	**Watch** Business not replaced over night, but can be over time - what is next in this business model?
Operational Excellence & People	**Lower** No economies of scale with customization; need higher people metrics	**Highest IVS** Efficiency is critical, Six Sigma/Lean is paramount.	**Medium** Need high scores on people metrics, ops metrics naturally lower.	**Medium** Need to create motivation and urgency to deliver in an environment that lacks competition.
Financial	**Watch** Too high levels of customization can lead to unprofitability.	**Medium** Just in time investments are the norm; balance of customer prices with costs.	**Watch** This is the constant tension and battle - Need ROA, ROE, but need to invest to get new hits.	**Highest IVS** Maximize returns while in a dominant position.

same industry, same geography, same size, and so on. This will at least give you a general gauge of where you rank compared to those other firms.

Comparisons beyond that are likely to be noise and not have much value. Trying to interpolate a firm's value or future value isn't what the total IVS score is intended for, and it will quickly deteriorate into a nonvalue-added conversation.

Categorical IVS Scores

The categorical IVS scores for customer, operations, growth, and financial are also good for similar comparability to the composite score, such as comparing business units internally or comparing categorical scores to similar firms based on demographics. These categorical scores have more meaning in that you can see "best-in-class" levels that other companies are attaining. If that category is part of your strategic value proposition (e.g., the growth category is significant to a company that has a strategic archetype of product developer), then you can use that to gauge if you need to bolster your efforts to get better results or if you are within a reasonable range in that particular category.

Individual IVS Scores by Metric

These individual scores are like most other benchmarks you have used. They can help you set goals and targets for what you want to achieve in your own business as well as give you meaningful targets to shoot for. Keep in mind, however, that many of the ratings in these benchmarks are general business benchmarks that do not take industry nuances into account. Consequently, you may need to ratchet up or down your expectations for these benchmarks, though they are still useful for comparisons to drive results.

> **Getting the resultant metrics is good—taking action from that information is paramount!**

 Where do you see value in comparability? IMA asked this question in its survey. The percentages below show what respondents felt would be the *most important* dimensions in benchmarking their organization's results with other companies and/or best-in-class metrics:

- 74%: Industry

- 58%: Strategic archetype (Low/Best price leader, Product developer, Custom solutions provider, and Proprietary leader)

- 57%: Company size based on annual revenues

- 40%: Geographical region (United States, Asia, Europe, etc.)

- 37%: Company type (Private, Public, etc.)

Industry usually tends to get top billing as the most relevant cut when comparing and contrasting your company's data and metrics against others. This research was no different. *Strategic archetype* ranked very high, but that also spoke to the value people saw in being able to compare against a similar strategic company, regardless of industry. They wanted to know who was truly best at getting results in a similar business approach and the levels they are achieving. *Company size, geography,* and *company type* were also all relevant, desired dimensions for comparability.

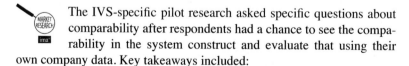 The IVS-specific pilot research asked specific questions about comparability after respondents had a chance to see the comparability in the system construct and evaluate that using their own company data. Key takeaways included:

1. *How valuable would it be to compare your organization's IVS scores with those of* similar companies *(i.e., same industry, size, geographic region, etc.; company names not listed)?*

a. *Not valuable*   *0%*

b. *Somewhat valuable*   *16%*

c. *Moderately valuable*   *13%*

d. **Very valuable**   **42%**

e. **Extremely valuable**   **29%**

2. *How valuable would it be to compare your organization's IVS scores with those of* all companies *regardless of industry (company names not listed)?*

a. *Not valuable*   *3%*

b. *Somewhat valuable*   *27%*

c. ***Moderately valuable***   ***40%***

d. *Very valuable*   *23%*

e. *Extremely valuable*   *7%*

There is a clear desire for the ability to compare results to similar companies. That kind of comparison—whether the companies are similar in industry, size, geography, or strategic archetype—provides relevance. Yes, sometimes you want to know and understand what is best in class regardless of those (or other) factors, but more often than not companies in the process of setting expectations and realistic goals are most concerned with what their competition and similar-profile companies look like.

REPORTING RESULTS AND TAKING ACTIONS

There are multiple reports that you can access to review your IVS trends and benchmarks. Most important, you also can review *where to take actions*. After all, you should be measuring things to improve them, so let's keep innovating and driving to create more innovation value. Even if you don't use the system, I'd like to capture here the concepts behind some of the reporting to emphasize what you can be and should be looking for when you calculate your IVS—and what you can do with the associated results.

- **BASIC reporting** is provided that renders your overall IVS composite score, your four categorical scores, and your individual

(16–24) IVS scores—all in a BSC format. This summary reporting tends to be a starting point for executive, and sometimes employee, reporting.

- **DEMOGRAPHICS reporting** is provided so you can compare and contrast your business against others, both similar and different. Many times it's helpful and more meaningful to compare against similar companies, but it is also helpful to take those demographic filters off occasionally and look at the best-in-class metrics regardless of demographics. That way, you can continue to challenge your business to get past industry-leading levels and get to best-in-class levels.

- **TRENDING reporting** is provided to look at your IVS scores over various time periods. While there is value and merit in the composite score and individual scores at any given time, one of your key goals should simply be to improve the metrics from one time period to the next. Improving the scores over time is just as, if not more, important than absolute scoring and reporting.

- **PORTOFOLIO BALANCE reporting** is provided so that you can see metrics that depict results in incremental, distinctive, and breakthrough areas. While you want to be monitoring and controlling that balance at a project level in your business, it is also helpful to categorize the metrics in that fashion to get a barometer reading on where and how you are spending your resources and on where you should focus.

- **PREDICTIONS reporting** is provided to look at lead vs. lag indicators. The 24 metrics are divided by lead or lag and are intended to give you some leading indicators that should help predict what type of lag results you should expect. Both kinds of metrics are obviously important, but giving a keen focus on lead indicators should help give you a sense of future payoffs.

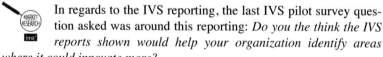 In regards to the IVS reporting, the last IVS pilot survey question asked was around this reporting: *Do you the think the IVS reports shown would help your organization identify areas where it could innovate more?*

Yes—93%

No—7%

It was gratifying to see that pilot participants could see value in the reports and use them in their company to help drive more innovation value.

Again, even if you don't use the IVS system, you can still have discussions around these concepts within your business and leadership teams.

FINAL THOUGHTS ON IVS

Earlier chapters and the innovation research conducted by IMA point to a simple realization: *We understand innovation and its value to our business, but it's hard to measure*. Through the creation of IVS, I have tried to balance multiple factors and address measuring innovation by an acceptable method.

First, I strove to come up with a meaningful measurement and management system for innovation. Second, I strove to come up with something that is easily understood—simple, but not simplistic. This is where I hope the utilization of a familiar tool like the BSC aids in the adoption and utilization of IVS. Third, I sought comparability with others. Many of us believe that competition is healthy and good. Competition drives performance and creates more value. If you can compare and contrast your innovation scores and results, you can determine where you should be more competitive, what levels are acceptable in specific areas, and where to make investments or course corrections. APQC and general benchmarks for specific metrics are helpful in this comparability. If you can see how others in both similar and dissimilar industries are achieving IVS results, you will be better armed.

Although it may not be easy to measure innovation at first, it's an important endeavor that you must embark on to drive more innovation value creation in your business.

ACTION: Before proceeding to the Final Thoughts and Appendix, use the following form to reflect on the measurement chapters, the third and final element of your Innovation Elixir. What were your key takeaways, and how will you customize these tools and principles to drive value in your company? Again, consider the trees from Part IV, but not at the peril of seeing the forest!

replace with
LOGO

GOLD NUGGETS
APPLICATION AT MY BUSINESS

THREE Gold Nuggets you are taking away as foundational elements of your innovation strategy, items for discussion and contemplation at your business with your teams, or concepts that need further research: *(circle one)*

1. *FOUNDATIONAL / DISCUSS / RESEARCH* _____

2. *FOUNDATIONAL / DISCUSS / RESEARCH* _____

3. *FOUNDATIONAL / DISCUSS / RESEARCH* _____

Concept to Execution → which concepts will I implement at our business?

Implement Immediately: **Reserve/Consider Later**

A. _____   C. _____

B. _____   D. _____

Innovation Elixir – The Secret Potion at My Business.

What specific tweaks would I need to make to achieve success at my business, with its unique culture, employees & leadership?

1. _____

2. _____

3. _____

Final Thoughts

You miss 100% of the shots you never take.
— Wayne Gretzky

As we come to an end on this innovation discussion, I hope this journey has enlightened you and given you some guidance that you can immediately apply to your organization. I hope the research conducted by IMA and included in this book provides relevant insights about the call to action and highlights how we all need to be engaged in supporting and driving innovation value in our respective organizations. Our markets and customers are morphing quickly and constantly, and we need to adapt our value propositions in how we deliver value to our customers. We each need to create our own, custom Innovation Elixir to drive and realize innovation value. I'd like to address these final thoughts in two categories: Stories of Lessons Learned and Critical Takeaways for Advancing Innovation.

STORIES OF LESSONS LEARNED

I have failed at about as many things as I've succeeded at in my career. That is why I've had some success—because I dared to fail. I can't say it was always fun, but, in retrospect, it was usually worth it. I remember reading a Russian expression once, which says: *"The wise man learns from someone else's mistakes, the smart man learns from his own, and the stupid one never learns."* It's smart to learn from your own mistakes, but it's wise to learn from other's mistakes so that you don't have to make as many in the first place.

As you are leading, mentoring, and teaching others to drive innovation in your leadership role, consider using storytelling as a way to convey knowledge. Storytelling via parables has been used for hundreds of generations. Telling stories that "stick," that people remember, is critical! *I hope you find gold nuggets within these final 10 stories of best practices and "mistakes":*

1. **Surround yourself with a great team** and other people who stretch their boundaries and have had their own share of successes and failures—collectively, you will get synergies. Build trust in your teams quickly, and you may be surprised at the speed of execution when you have high levels of trust and camaraderie in place. I have very intentionally put this as the first lesson learned. I have had some great teams and teammates, and I've had some that didn't fit—and

many of us tend to take too long to swap out players that don't fit. Don't make this classic mistake! Get the right players on board and enable them to do great things!

2. **Ensure you have good advisors in your life.** I believe everyone would benefit from a personal board of directors or advisors to guide them in facets of their life, and I think many of us do this informally. One of my insights in this realm came from *Thinkertoys* by Michael Michalko, which suggests having a Hall of Fame of advisors, both real and fictional, to consult the world's great minds for inspiration, balance, guidance, advice, and insight.

I've created my own Hall of Fame of great thinkers, which I've posted on my office wall so that I can refer to it when I need insight or guidance. I'm sharing my list of personal advisors with you so you can see if and how this could help you—either in your innovation governance journey or your personal journeys. Consider making a list like this for yourself that you can turn to for advice and counsel. I'd also suggest a "real, living" board of advisors you can literally talk to, but this Hall of Fame advisors board can also be helpful to stretch your thinking. I hope you enjoy my list of advisors (listed alphabetically), the role in which they play, and a memorable quote from them:

a. **Aristotle,** *Philosopher***:** *"Courage is the first of human qualities because it is the quality which guarantees the others."*

b. **Marcus Aurelius,** *Leader:* *"The true worth of a man is to be measured by the objects he pursues."*

c. **Thomas Edison,** *Inventor***:** *"I have not failed. I've just found 10,000 ways that won't work."*

d. **Ralph Waldo Emerson,** *Poet***:** *"Nothing great was ever achieved without enthusiasm."*

e. **Steve Jobs,** *Innovator***:** *"The only way to do great work is to love what you do."*

f. **Martin Luther King,** *Activist***:** *"I have a dream…"*

g. **Abraham Lincoln,** *Leader***:** *"I destroy my enemies when I make them my friends."*

h. **Sun Tzu,** *Strategist***:** *"Every battle is won before it is fought."*

If you had to pick one company that you would describe as being successful in innovation and driving innovation value, Apple would be on the top of many people's lists. I have never worked at Apple, but I've read a lot about the company, watched it for many years, and have used many of its products. I couldn't even guess the number of Apple products I have in my house based on my family's tech appetite and usage. The next four lessons are illustrations of Apple, but many other companies have similar stories.

3. **Recognize that people care about the experience they have with your product.** How many people have told you they love their iPhone? Quite a few, I bet. People *love* their iPhone. Why? Because they can do a great deal with it, it can be fun, it is intuitive to use, and the list goes on. Apple spends a tremendous amount of time thinking about *how* the customer will use its products and how the customer's *experience* can be improved. When is the last time you heard someone say they *loved* their Blackberry? (Sorry, Blackberry.) Yet at one point, almost everyone in corporate America seemed to have one—and they hated it! Funny thing, the Blackberry phones did many of the same things that iPhones do, but the experience was totally different.

   People pay for a great user experience, and today they demand it or vote with their feet—walking right out the door to buy a competitor's product. Do you consider the experience your customer will have with your product? When is the last time you listened to customer calls or talked directly with a client to hear his or her feedback? Sometimes we can get so busy running our companies that we forget about taking care of our customers and managing and improving the experience they have with us.

4. **Have a balanced portfolio.** When Apple started out, it had only one product: the Apple IIe. Remember those? I remember as a kid playing "Oregon Trail" on the school's computer, and I thought it was incredible. Little did I realize the future of computers and gaming systems. Later, Apple, like many companies that matured, moved from an organization that focused on a single product to a company with a full portfolio of offerings.

   Fast forward to today, and look at the various products, services, and offerings that Apple has in play. Consider a traditional product lifecycle curve or an S-curve, and think about the products and services that Apple has and where they could be depicted on that curve. Currently, the company has products in full maturity, like the iPhone and the Mac. It has products in the decline phase, such as the iPod. It has products in the introduction phase, such as the Apple Watch, and I'm sure the company has numerous products in the pipeline phase for future release.

   What's the point? Apple has an array of products and services in the development stages that it is experimenting with and may later bring to market. It doesn't have its entire future pinned to one product. Apple has products and services in all phases of growth, from incubation to maturity and even decline.

Sometimes the hardest thing for mature companies to do is deciding which products, services, or markets they need to sunset and exit from. Sometimes a thoughtful exit in a declining market is one of the best moves you can make, freeing up those resources to use on a new product, service, or market. Ultimately, you need to have a balanced portfolio to survive and thrive in today's fast-paced market. While some of our markets and industries move faster or slower than others, they all move. And you would be well-served to consider the balance of products and services in your portfolio.

5. **One person can't be the sole innovator.** I admire Steve Jobs. I think he had an incredibly innovative mind and mind-set, and his impact will long be felt. I never had the opportunity to meet him, so I can't personally say many things for sure about him, but I can make some deductions that I believe are relevant.

One is that not many companies have a Steve Jobs anywhere within their company, and that actually may be a good thing. Why? Because one person can't be the sole innovator or ideas person. Innovation is a team sport, remember? The best leaders and the most successful companies create innovation value by harnessing the thinking, creativity, ideas, and execution of as *many* constituents (employees, partnerships, suppliers, and so on) as possible. Would I like to have a Steve Jobs in my business? Absolutely yes! But you need to have more than one person coming up with ideas in your innovation endeavors.

I would suggest that in Jobs's second tenure with Apple, he created more of an innovation culture and related governance structure, and he wasn't the sole ideas guy that he was known for earlier in his career. He was still an innovator and inventor, but I believe he worked hard to drive that deeper into his team and others. I believe he created more of a culture in which all could innovate and thrive.

6. **Give the people what they want, even if they don't know what they want.** This is a tall order, but somehow Apple seems to do it pretty consistently. Apple seems to find ways to give people things they didn't even know they wanted or needed. I think some of this is done merely through talking with customers, then imagining how they can help those people with what they want (e.g., using focus groups). Many of the oft-repeated quotes from Steve Jobs revolve

around doing things for customers: being customer-centric, being relentless in delivering value to the customer, and creating an experience that is superior.

I think some of Apple's success comes from a position of being willing to fail. The company knows that not all of its new product launches will be the next Mac or iPhone. Yet it keeps taking shots. And when it fails, which it does, it learns from the failures and adjusts as it goes forward.

Talk to your customers, but apply your insights and talents to what you can deliver better than anyone else!

7. **Technology in agriculture: when to embrace, and when to wait.** Consider small family farms in the U.S. during the 1950s through the 1970s. As technology advances came fast and furious, the family farmer needed to decide which technologies to embrace right away, which they should let become more mature, and which they should dismiss all together. Take out the word "farming," and you could apply this to almost any business today. Many of us struggle with adopting new technology and timing in our respective industries. It isn't an easy task and decision. For farmers, this mostly came down to a simple payback analysis. "How much of my profits would I need to invest on the new technology, and what savings or incremental revenues would I reap?" Additionally, specifically applicable to farming, payback period is important. Even with a high return on investment, if the payback period is several years and you have a bad growing season, a bird flu epidemic, foot and mouth disease in cattle, or some other anomaly, could you hold on long enough to recoup your investment costs and actually get to the cost savings or additional revenue-producing phase before going bankrupt? It's sad to think that many small farmers went out of business on both ends of this decision. Some adopted new technology too slowly or not at all and simply could not keep pace with the new economic model of farming that involved larger-scale farmers producing more and getting better yields and economies of scale. On the flip side, some farmers racing to the leading edge of technology simply invested too much too fast. When that was done during a period of skyrocketing land prices or plummeting crop prices, those results were catastrophic and created many bankruptcies. The timing of technology adoption and the payback period of that investment is not a decision to take lightly.

With technology and innovation, always remember the adage "measure twice, cut once." That is, be very thoughtful, deliberate, and careful about how and when you implement new technology.

Find the balance of not too slow and not too fast—which is, obviously, easier said than done.

8. **Alliances, partnerships, and co-ops—aligning interests.** Partnerships and co-op farming is a classic value chain discussion. That's the case regardless of industry, but let's consider a farming example to make this real. Co-ops are formed by farmers as a way to get better pricing and buying power with suppliers, such as seed manufacturers for planting their crops, as well as combining products like milk to get the best market price. Co-ops in farming can serve as a simple yet fundamental example for many of our own businesses. Don't do it alone if you can create leverage and economies of scale via partnerships, co-ops, joint ventures, and the like. Sometimes those that appear to be your competitors in the market can actually be your allies, and through partnerships and agreements you can create more value together than you can achieve separately. It's Economics 101—consider supply and demand: partner to create value.

9. *Mise en place* **enables execution and success**! We are pivoting from the world of agriculture to the culinary scene for these last two stories of lessons learned. Do you know what *mise en place* means in the culinary world? It means everything is in its place. Do you know what separates many good chefs from great chefs and successful restaurant services from failures? *Mise en place*! *Mise en place* is all about being prepared. Have you ever watched a cooking show or demonstration? If you haven't, it's simple; the chef is in a demo kitchen showing you how to prepare some fabulous meal and explaining along the way how to execute key steps. And they always make it look *so easy*, don't they?! Something that would take the average home cook an hour or more to prepare seems to take the professional about 12 minutes! Why? Because the chef prepared many things ahead of time. Think back to that cooking demo: Everything is in place before the chef smiles for the camera and says, "Bonjour." The ovens are preheated, the vegetables chopped, the proteins carved or prepped, the ingredients premeasured, and the cooking vessels and tools needed to prepare the entrée are at hand. Think about all the work that went into that cooking demo before the first step in the recipe execution was even shown to you on camera! Envisioning the end product, everything was planned out and set up for success. Now, don't get me wrong, the chef still needs to execute, and that skill and execution is critical, but he or she is already set up for success and should be better able to rebound if something goes wrong in the execution phase because of that preparation. In our environments in business, can

we prepare for everything that may happen when we are executing? No. But we can prepare for successful execution ahead of time, much like that chef does. That frees us up to focus on execution and make adjustments as needed in real time while executing the plan. A little thoughtful planning goes a long, long way. Every game is partially won before you ever take the field. Preparation is key!

10. **More ingredients on the plate aren't always better!** This is hard for some chefs to accept. But many of the best ones get it, embody it, and showcase it. I think many people can take fabulous, expensive ingredients in the kitchen, like filet mignon and lobster, and create a great dish. But the great chefs take rather pedestrian ingredients and elevate them to a whole new level. As a chef myself, people often ask me, "What is your favorite dish to prepare?" The simple answer is, "It depends." It depends what season it is, what proteins and produce are fresh and available, and what kind of mood I'm in—or better said, how creative I feel.

Let's use one of my classical favorites, chicken chasseur. The recipe is simple: chicken, some basic vegetables, and seasonings. Can that be made extraordinary? Absolutely! The levels of flavor you can create in this dish with some basic ingredients (and some chef skills) is amazing, leading to a delectable dish. So what is the lesson? You don't need to have 50 components on a plate for it to be a spectacular dish, nor do you need to use the most expensive ingredients. Similarly, you don't need to have 50 bells, whistles, and features on your product to make it spectacular. When you are designing or reinventing a product, think about a chef's dish. Are you trying too hard to be fancy and creating something with a bunch of components that don't really go together, or are you being a classical chef and creating something with high value by combining the critical components only and elevating it to a new level for your customers? Sometimes less is more, and there is value and joy in simplicity.

The stories of these lessons learned not only support the concepts discussed throughout the book, but they're also meant to underscore the idea that you should make it a habit—a constant process—to learn from the success and failures of others. Think of it as a variation of Proudly Discovered Elsewhere. Always look to others for what they have learned and apply it to your own situation and business to drive value. You can't get insights unless you ask—take the time and opportunity to ask! And you can't learn if you don't have your eyes open looking for new things!

CRITICAL TAKEAWAYS FOR ADVANCING INNOVATION

I view everything in this book as important, or I wouldn't have included it. But I want to end with five final takeaways from this book. Here are the five keys I hope you have discovered:

1. **Innovation governance is a yin and yang relationship**. Apply them in the proportions that make sense in your business. It may not be a 50/50 proportion, and it's you job as a leader figure that out. But regardless of proportion, apply them both—creativity and ideation with discipline and execution to drive innovation value!

2. **Remember the three elements of innovation execution**: *Galvanize* your organization and prepare it for success; *enable* your organization by implementing multiple innovation channels to solicit, collect, evaluate, and implement ideas; and *measure* innovation value within your company and against others in your industry and geography and against those that are best in class. Create the optimal Innovation Elixir® for your business—remember the base elements, then add new ingredients and vary the composition to create that perfect concoction that will work in your business to achieve innovation value.

3. **You can't improve something if you can't measure it**. Use the Innovation Value Score® (IVS) to measure innovation progress and value in your company and as a yardstick to measure and compare with other companies to collectively raise your innovation game and achieve more innovation value. Remember, the end-game isn't the actual calculation results of IVS; it's what you do with those results—how you better align resources, processes, and metrics to achieve your strategic plans and vision. Establish your strategy and targets, measure the results, then discuss and debate where you want to make improvements to your value proposition through innovation.

4. **You don't need to be Steve Jobs to facilitate innovation in your organization**. As a matter of fact, some of the best facilitators, enablers, and leaders of innovation come up with few ideas themselves, but they empower and create the conditions for others to innovate and be successful in their business. You may be incredibly positioned and uniquely skilled to facilitate, lead, and support innovative efforts in your business. Remember to engage others to help you lead and support innovation—it's a team sport!

5. **My last takeaway comes in the form of a quote from Walt Disney**: "*If you can dream it, you can do it.*" Nothing can take the place of action and experimentation. Dream it, then get into the scrum! Make a play, test a theory, trial a product, talk with a customer—do something that has a potential to create value!

Innovation governance is needed, balance is needed, and execution is needed. But sometimes one of the simple ingredients missing is inspiration. Inspire others to innovate! Get employees, suppliers, customers, and other stakeholders excited about your business and collectively strive to make it better. You have the skills and ability to do this!

Good luck in your execution of innovation and creating innovation value!

Appendix

IMA SURVEY ON INNOVATION

IMA received a total of 271 responses to the survey. The tables below show the full results of the survey, including the demographic information of the respondents.

Raw Response Data

1. Please indicate your level of agreement with the following statements (Strongly Agree, Agree, Neutral, Disagree, Strongly Disagree):

	SA (%)	A (%)	N (%)	D (%)	SD (%)	Blank (%)	Total (%)
Innovation *is* a key focus in my organization's overall strategy.	26.6	40.2	22.9	9.2	1.1	0.0	100.0
Innovation *should be* a key focus in my organization's overall strategy.	57.2	34.7	6.3	0.7	1.1	0.0	100.0
If I were asked to provide innovation governance leadership (i.e., support, leadership, direction), I would feel comfortable and knowledgeable in doing so.	19.2	42.8	26.6	10.0	1.1	0.4	100.0
My organization sets innovation goals.	12.9	30.6	27.7	24.0	3.0	1.8	100.0
My organization generally wants to innovate, but short-term financial risks and goals get in the way.	11.4	35.8	25.1	25.1	2.2	0.4	100.0
Innovation measures are used in performance reviews in my organization.	7.4	27.3	24.4	33.6	5.9	1.5	100.0

2. Where do you need the *most* innovation improvement and support?

	No.	%
Galvanizing: Training and educating the organization for innovation success (e.g., cultural readiness, common innovation language, clear leadership expectations, and an overall excitement to innovate).	36	13.3
Enabling: Implementing multiple innovation channels to solicit, capture, provide funding for, evaluate, execute, and report on innovation projects/ideas.	38	14.0
Measurement: Measuring innovation value created on a regular basis to compare progress internally or within an industry and to identify alignment of innovation value creation to business strategies.	28	10.3
All of the above	161	59.4
No answer	8	3.0
Total	271	100.0

3. Where do you currently (or would like to) get innovation ideas and inputs from? (Check all that apply.)

	Currently (%)	Would like to (%)	Blank (%)	Total (%)
Employees via idea suggestions	52.0	43.2	4.8	100.0
Key employees who are charged with innovation and idea creation	56.5	39.5	4.1	100.0
Key suppliers	30.6	55.0	14.4	100.0
Customers	42.8	50.2	7.0	100.0
Competitors (fast follower strategy)	35.8	47.2	17.0	100.0
External agencies/consultants/ institutions	41.3	46.9	11.8	100.0

4. How do you currently measure innovation success/value?

	No.	%
We don't formally measure innovation success/value	153	56.5
Number of new products, services, and/or patents	43	15.9
Percentage of sales revenue from new products	39	14.4
Customer retention	22	8.1

Other	12	4.4
Blank	2	0.7
Total	271	100.0

5. How often are your senior finance and accounting leaders asked to help lead, support, or measure innovation efforts?

	Little/ None (%)	Somewhat (%)	Often (%)	Blank (%)	Total (%)
10 years ago	53.1	24.0	11.1	11.8	100.0
Today	28.4	41.3	25.5	4.8	100.0
In the next one to three years	17.3	35.8	38.0	8.9	100.0

6. Which processes do you think should include innovation discussion in your organization? (Select all that apply.)

	Selected	%
Budgeting	188	69.4
Capital planning	174	64.2
Operational reviews	187	69.0
Strategic planning, including risk and opportunity identification	237	87.5

7. Which of the following dimensions is/are *very* important when benchmarking your organization's results with other companies and/or best-in-class metrics? (Select all that apply.)

	Selected	%
Company size	153	56.5
Geographical region (United States, Asia, Europe, etc.)	108	39.9
Industry	201	74.2
Company type (private, public, etc.)	99	36.5
Type of strategy (low cost leader, product leader, custom solution provider, etc.)	156	57.6

8. If you had to split your innovation resources and time among the following three categories, how would you allocate resources at your company? *(Allocate 100% among the three.)*

	Min.	Max.	Mean	Median	Standard Deviation (%)
Incremental: Continuous improvement efforts driving efficiencies and improvements	0	100	41.0	40	21.0
Distinctive: Innovation projects that will add to your competitive advantage and value proposition (e.g., new products, offerings, etc.)	0	85	32.2	30	15.4
Breakthrough: New markets, big bets on new products, investments, etc.	0	80	22.8	20	15.1

9. How often would you say that your organization needs to significantly evolve or reinvent its business value proposition (i.e., create significantly new or different products, services, operational models)?

	No.	%
1–3 years	100	36.9
3–5 years	103	38.0
5–10 years	51	18.8
20+ years	17	6.3
Total	271	100.0

10. Do you think that your organization should measure and govern innovation regularly as a key business process to sustain growth and value?

	No.	%
Yes	250	92.3
No	20	7.4
Blank	1	0.4
Total	271	100.0

11. What is your job title?

	No.	%
Controller, financial controller, or comptroller	66	24.4
Finance or accounting manager	57	21.0
CFO	50	18.5
Finance director	28	10.3
Senior accountants	25	9.2
VP	21	7.7
Owner/partner	13	4.8
Executive officer	7	2.6
COO	4	1.5
Total	271	100.0

12. Industry. Which of the following best describes your organization?

	No.	%
Manufacturing: Aerospace, Automotive, all other Manufacturing	80	29.5
Business Services: Advertising, Banking, Consulting, Financial Services, Legal, Publishing	46	17.0
Institutions: Government, Education, Not-for-Profit	32	11.8
Retail: Apparel, Consumer Packaged Goods (CPG), Wholesale/Retail	26	9.6
Technology: Biotech, Computer, Software, Technology, Telecom	18	6.6
Healthcare: Facilities, Payers, Providers, Supporting Products and Services	12	4.4
Other	55	20.3
Not answered	2	0.7
Total	271	100.0

13. Location. Where is your business unit primarily located?

	No.	%
United States	138	50.9
Middle East	65	24.0
Asia/Pacific	45	16.6
Europe	13	4.8

Africa	6	2.2
Canada	3	1.1
Not answered	1	0.4
Total	271	100.0

14. Revenues. What is your organization's annual revenues (or budget, if it's a nonprofit or governmental entity) in U.S. dollars?

	No.	%
$0–$5 million	47	17.5
$5 million–$100 million	104	38.8
$100 million–$1 billion	52	19.4
$1 billion–$5 billion	28	10.4
$5 billion+	37	13.8
Total	268	100.0

Innovation Value Score®

15. Would you be willing to complete the Innovation Value Score metrics and evaluation?

	No.	%
Yes	161	59.4
No	110	40.6
Total	271	100.0

TEMPLATES AND REPORTS

Throughout this book, I've given you multiple insights and references on how to implement and execute innovation governance. That's a start, but you still need to interpret the direction and insights so you can apply them to your business. To help jumpstart that process and give you a leg up on getting to better innovation governance in a faster time frame, I'm including the following forms that you can download and use. In buying this book, you are also entitled to access and use the following forms and templates. This appendix highlights the forms, their use, and give some examples.

The digital copies of the forms can be found on the Templates tab of www.innovationvaluescore.com. They have been conveniently set up so that you can insert your company logo and begin using them immediately! You are also encouraged to change the forms to best fit your business and accompanying culture. I offer these forms as a best practice, but even best practices need to be tweaked to take into account specific dynamics and cultural aspects in any business. So download the forms, tweak them to your liking and needs, and good luck with driving more and better innovation governance to ultimately create more innovation value!

Chapter Summaries: Gold Nugget Takeaways

replace with
LOGO

GOLD NUGGETS
APPLICATION AT MY BUSINESS

THREE Gold Nuggets you are taking away as foundational elements of your innovation strategy, items for discussion and contemplation at your business with your teams, or concepts that need further research: *(circle one)*

1. *FOUNDATIONAL / DISCUSS / RESEARCH* _____

2. *FOUNDATIONAL / DISCUSS / RESEARCH* _____

3. *FOUNDATIONAL / DISCUSS / RESEARCH* _____

Concept to Execution → which concepts will I implement at our business?

Implement Immediately: **Reserve/Consider Later**

A. _____   C. _____

B. _____   D. _____

Innovation Elixir – The Secret Potion at My Business.

What specific tweaks would I need to make to achieve success at my business, with its unique culture, employees & leadership?

1. _____

2. _____

3. _____

Form Importance: While you read this book, use this form to capture your thoughts on the gold nuggets you are taking away from the content and discussion, what you want to execute, and how you need to tweak the concept or content to be the most effective in your business. You can certainly use this form and template for many other uses as well. Pull out this form whenever you come across a new book, new model, new methodology, and so forth and want to capture your critical thoughts. Also, this is a great form to hand out to your staff or teams if you want to get independent feedback on a concept/method and then consolidate the feedback for discussion.

Nuances: You are using this form in a "diverging/converging" format of getting feedback and then having a discussion. In the converging part of that discussion, how you tweak the concept/method to make it work in your business with your employees is the real secret sauce to the discussion. Lots of people have models and tools that work in THEIR companies. The trick is how to make it work in YOUR company!

RACI Form for Innovation

replace with
LOGO

INNOVATION RACI

Ln	Column1	Innovation Leader	CEO	Executive Team	Department Managers	Employees	Customers	Suppliers	<blank>	<blank>2	Key notes
1	Creates innovation roadmap of strategies, channels/mechanisms, milestones and timelines	A	R	R	I	I	-	-	-	-	*Must have responsibility across the executive leadership team for success*
2	Monitors and reviews innovation reporting	A	R	R	I	I	-	-	-	-	
3	Submits innovation ideas, responses to business challenges	R	-	I	A	A	A	A	-	-	*The innovaiton leader is not the ideas person. Yes, they can contribute but they are not the sole idea generator.*
4	Evaluates innovation ideas and business challenge submissions	A	I, C	R, I		I	I	I	-	-	*CEO consulted on business challenge topics; Executive team rotates responsibility for evaluation and monitoring depending on area impacted.*
5	Leads and produces results from Future Sensing Group	A, R	I, C	I, C	-	R	-	-	-	-	*Those employees selected to the FSG are responsible*
6	Leads and produces results from Crowdsourcing	A, R	I, C	I, C	-	-	R, C	R, C	-	-	
7	Evaluates, sponsors and monitors Fellowship program	A, R	I, C	R, I	R	I			-	-	*Department managers are responsible to support the chosen individuals and backfill their work freeing them up to execute the fellowship.*
8											
9											
10											

R = Responsibile
A = Accountable
C = Consulted
I = Informed

Form Importance: The RACI form delineates who is Responsible, Accountable, Consulted, and Informed because it is important to clearly define innovation roles and responsibilities across the leadership team and entire business.

Nuances:

1. The Innovation Leader column is critical and has to be updated with what the CEO has empowered that person to do. This also is a helpful tool with which to negotiate and stress the importance of RACI roles for yourself as the leader and for the entire executive team.

2. Add other constituents in the blank columns as you delineate your employee population or other constituents. For example, if you are a nonprofit, you may have a volunteer board of directors that is very active in the business. They should have a clear role in innovation.

3. See the "key notes" on the form for additional nuances that you may want to share with your CEO and executive team for discussion.

Innovation Foundation Readiness Checklist

FOUNDATION READINESS CHECKLIST

Input a score of 1-5: **1** = None / No **2** = Little **3** = Moderate **4** = Good **5** = Excellent	
QUESTION	SCORE
1. CEO supports innovation	3
2. Executive Leadership team is committed to support innovation	3
3. An innovation roadmap (strategies, goals, timelines, expected results) is prepared and ready for execution	3
4. There is clear alignment of innovation initiatives to existing business processes like budgeting, capital planning, operations reviews, etc.	3
5. We have created monitoring and measuring systems/methods with which to evaluate and report on innovation value created.	3
6. We have clear communication channels with which to share innovation results with employees, customers, suppliers and the market in general.	3
7. We have designed appropriate incentives and rewards for innovation submission and value creation.	3
8. Departmental goals have been/will be cascaded throughout the organization to drive results and ensure accountability.	3
9. Learning and training tools are accessible to all employees	3
10. Our culture is ready for innovation - they understand they can fail, but need to learn fast and continue to find ways to drive innovation value for our customers.	3
Total Score:	30

Scores = 0 - 19: STOP – remediate these items before proceeding
Scores = 21 - 34: Consider more galvanizing steps prior to execution
Scores = 35+: GO - EXECUTE!

Form Importance: This form is meant to provide a barometer to gauge if your business is ready to launch, invigorate, or accept an innovation initiative or focus. Galvanizing the organization is critical before you attempt to drive innovation value creation and results. While you can't amass any value until you begin executing, you need to prepare the organization properly or your execution may be for naught. And many times it can be harder to start a program or effort the second time after an unsuccessful launch. Thoughtfully consider these ratings and determine if you need to shore up any areas prior to implementing specific innovation channels.

Nuances:

1. You may need to add more factors that you deem necessary to evaluate your business's readiness.

2. Try to evaluate and answer these questions as accurately as possible; don't be overly optimistic (possibly setting you up for failure) or overly pessimistic (possibly costing you time in getting results).

3. Get multiple leaders or employees to fill out this form and compare results. While this is a self-assessment, it is important to get that assessment from multiple data points to ensure results.

Portfolio Balance Template

replace with
LOGO

Portfolio of Innovation Projects

	Costs	Benefits	% of Total Costs	% of Total Benefits	Benefit Area:	IVS Metric Impacted
Incremental						
<insert project name>	$ 1	$ 1				
<insert project name>	$ 1	$ 1				
insert rows above this line						
subtotal - Incremental Projects:	$ 2	$ 2	33%	33%		
Distinctive						
<insert project name>	$ 1	$ 1				
<insert project name>	$ 1	$ 1				
insert rows above this line						
subtotal - Distinctive Projects:	$ 2	$ 2	33%	33%		
Breakthrough						
<insert project name>	$ 1	$ 1				
<insert project name>	$ 1	$ 1				
insert rows above this line						
subtotal - Breakthrough Projects:	$ 2	$ 2	33%	33%		
Total Project Investments / Benefits	$ 6	$ 6				

Form Importance: Balance is important as you track and review your portfolio of innovation projects, including intentional strategic imbalances that match your strategy. Remember Chapter 5's baseball analogy of winning the game through hitting singles, doubles, triples, *and* home runs.

Nuances:

1. The balance is subjective to your business and its level of maturity and overall value propositions. You do need a balance and have to determine the best mix for your business at any given point in time. If you have an imbalance, take that approach with your eyes wide open and in agreement with the team.

2. While time frames aren't listed on the form, you should definitely consider them, such as the length of time it will take to bring new products or enhancements to market. Again, this is a balance between delivering things in the next month, next quarter, and next year and having a couple of longer-term plays in the portfolio. They can't all be long term or short term.

Open Innovation Submission Template

replace with
LOGO

OPEN INNOVATION
SUBMISSION

GENERAL

NAME

                                            Last   First

DEPARTMENT

CONTACT

                                            Phone   Email

STATEMENT OF IDEA

INVESTMENT

| COST ESTIMATE | $ | | VALUE ESTIMATE | $ |

KEY IMPLEMENTATION STEPS

1
2
3
4
5

Would you like to be involved in implementation?   ⊙ Yes   ○ No

INNOVATION GOVERNANCE SECTION

| ASSIGNED EVALUATOR | | DISPOSITION | ☐ Explore
☐ Pass
☐ Hold |

DISPOSITION RATIONALE

☐ Yes, proceed with exploration
☐ Yes, likely, but needs refinement
☐ 50-50, could go either way

☐ No, already attempted or in place
☐ No, cost prohibitive
☐ No, not aligned with company mission/vision

Form Importance: Setting up an Open Innovation Submission channel is supposed to be easy. But it isn't always easy to make something simple. Take great care in the design of this form in order to provide a channel to get simple innovation ideas and feedback. Have a few minimalistic parameters so that you get some basic information in the submissions and more than just half-baked ideas. (Refer back to Chapter 6 for more information on this channel.)

Nuances:

1. Company culture! Keep this form simple, but give considerable thought to your business culture and environment and how this channel (and form) will be received.

2. Details vs. brevity. Details provide relevant information and deeper thinking than just making a simple suggestion—hold the employees accountable to think more and not just complain (that is, "bring me a solution, not a problem"). But requiring too many details take time and effort and may stifle submissions. Brevity gets more ideas but can result in not enough thinking on a full solution. Balance this dichotomy carefully, and don't be scared to try different things to see how much you can push in either direction.

3. Anonymous vs. named submitters. Putting a "name" on the form is good if you need to ask clarifying questions, give recognition, or say thank you. But sometimes people may want to submit an idea anonymously. Consider if and how you want to accommodate that on this form or if you want to capture anonymous inputs via another process or mechanism like an employee satisfaction instrument.

Business Challenge Template

replace with
LOGO   **BUSINESS CHALLENGE**

GENERAL

NAME (CAPTAIN)

Last	*First*

DEPARTMENT

CONTACT

Phone	*Email*

TEAM MEMBERS

MEMBER NAMES (FOR TEAM CHALLENGES ONLY)

1	*Last*	*First*
2	*Last*	*First*
3	*Last*	*First*
4	*Last*	*First*
5	*Last*	*First*

BUSINESS CHALLENGE TOPIC

BUSINESS CHALLENGE DETAILS/FACTS

1

2

3

4

5

BUSINESS CHALLENGE SOLUTION

INVESTMENT

COST ESTIMATE $ VALUE ESTIMATE $

KEY IMPLEMENTATION STEPS

1

2

3

4

5

Would you like to be involved in implementation?   ⦿ Yes   ○ No

INNOVATION GOVERNANCE SECTION

| ASSIGNED EVALUATOR | | DISPOSITION | ☐ Explore
 ☐ Pass
 ☐ Hold |

DISPOSITION RATIONALE

☐ Yes, proceed with exploration

☐ No, already attempted or in place
☐ No, cost prohibitive
☐ No, not aligned with company mission/vision
☐ Other

Form Importance: This form should be fun, exciting, and something employees look forward to seeing. Have a little "marketing flash" around it to make it enticing. (Refer back to Chapter 7 for more information on this innovation channel.)

Nuances:

1. The scope of the challenge is always the first consider. If the problem you pick is too big (i.e., so detailed that you need two pages to describe the problem), you have likely picked a bad topic. Use this form as a guideline to help ensure it doesn't get too long. If it does, it may not be the right challenge to use.

2. Be clear in the type of response you want. What kind of financial information, what type of action steps and at what level, and what considerations have they given? To get complete responses, don't overwhelm your participants with too many submission criteria and details. You don't want them choosing not to participate because of the complexity of the application.

Future Sensing Group Charter

FUTURE SENSING GROUP CHARTER

PURPOSE STATEMENT & TEAM OBJECTIVES

The purpose of this group is to norm, form and storm over innovation ideas, business challenges, industry and market turbulence and to take all this information and turn it into actionable decisions and recommendations.

MEMBERSHIP AND EXPECTATIONS

The Executive Team has discussed and chartered the formation of this group. We are excited to have some of our best thought leaders, executors and business experts come together to collectively work on business problems, idea improvements to our value proposition and offer insights and recommendations to the Executive Team. The following people have been carefully and specifically selected to participate in this group:

TEAM MEMBERS

MEMBER NAME

1			6		
	Last	First		Last	First
2			7		
	Last	First		Last	First
3			8		
	Last	First		Last	First
4			9		
	Last	First		Last	First
5			10		
	Last	First		Last	First

TEAM LEADER

Last	First

Expectations: The expectations for this team are simple. We expect the team members to attend scheduled team meetings and make meaningful contributions. Attendance of less than 70% of the scheduled meetings will lead to dismissal from the team – we want you to contribute! This is a one year commitment at which time you can request another year on the team or rotate off to free up a space for another leader to join.

TEAM PROCESS MANAGEMENT

This team will meet on a monthly basis with a predefined agenda and topics which the group will focus on. The team leader will consult with the Executive Team on topical areas and business issues along with our innovation roadmap to determine where this team can be most helpful and timely in providing insights and recommendations.

DECISION MAKING PROCEDURE

Decisions from this group will be governed by the team leader. Decisions and outcomes are expected to come in the following varieties:

- **Recommendations** – this group will be asked to render recommendations on various topics and issues to the executive team and the business in general. These recommendations will come in a consolidated format from the team as a whole, not individual reviews or feedback.
- **Evaluations** – at times this group will be asked to make a final decision on business aspects or issues. How these decisions are made will be discussed with your team leader who will determine the best process to get to a decision. Independent feedback and input will always be sought, but the group is to collective make decisions and support those decisions upon conclusion. Illustrative examples:
  - Who is the winner in a business challenge?
  - Pick the best idea to be implemented
  - Put these capital projects in rank order of importance.

TEAM COMMUNICATIONS

The main premise of this group is to create value through offering insights and recommendations to our executive leadership team. Many times this will mean working with confidential information, which many of you are used to already, and may also involve first-mover market advantages, so keeping strategies confidential is important. As a rule of thumb, you should consider all information, recommendations, and decisions to be confidential unless you have received permission from the team leader or specially been asked to communicate results to your functional areas.

EMPOWERMENT BOUNDARIES

The team is empowered to get _internal_ input and feedback through all their normal business channels and processes for the executive on Future Sensing Group activity. However, team members should consult the team leader prior to spending any time or resources on obtaining any additional, _external_ feedback or data. This is meant to eliminate redundancies or solicit data or input that may not be fully required. Also, consideration should be given such that we do not unnecessarily burden internal support teams with work associated to Future Sensing Group activity which may not be in full alignment with other activity and timelines.

TEAM FUNDING NEEDS

A majority of the work this team will be asked to do will not require additional funding outside of normal business funding and operations. However, if additional funds are needed for external information, rewards and incentives to drive employee results, external consultants and so forth, the team leader will work with Innovation Governance and request existing funds in that budget for the support and execution of this work.

PROCESS ROLES

This team will not have formal process roles of facilitator, timekeeper, notes taker, etc. Due to the makeup of this team and the high talent that is involved, we expect that you will share responsibilities and rotate team process roles as needed for maximum effectiveness and efficiency.

MEASUREMENT OF TEAM EFFECTIVENESS

The Team Leader and the full Executive Team will be responsible for providing feedback on team effectiveness. We encourage the team to develop self-measurement systems of how to predict and measure success. At minimum we will provide feedback at six-month and annual points to provide our feedback.

Form Importance: If you picked the right people for the FSG, they will self-govern. Without a team charter, however, they don't know the rules of the game. Think of this charter like telling a group of kids how to play soccer—you tell them the rules, how to score, what penalties are, and how to ultimately win. If you don't tell them the boundaries and rules, they are going to get frustrated and not know how to play. Tell them how to play! Also, this constitutes the assignment and agreement with your CEO and executive team as well as describing the expectations for participants. (Refer back to Chapter 8 for more information on this innovation channel.)

Nuances:

1. This charter is a fairly standard team charter template that has been modified to consider ways to get value and set parameters for an innovation group or Future Sensing Group. As with all forms and templates, it needs to be adjusted to match your company culture. In this case, also adjust the governance rules and procedures on authorities, decision making, communications, and so forth.

2. While you need to set the boundaries, try not to be overly restrictive. The charter shouldn't be more than two or three pages. It's intended to provide guidance and boundaries, not answers to every question they may ever conceivably come up against.

Fellowship Application

FELLOWSHIP APPLICATION

GENERAL

NAME

Last   *First*

DEPARTMENT

CONTACT

Phone   *Email*

STATEMENT OF FELLOWSHIP IDEA

INVESTMENT

COST ESTIMATE	$		VALUE ESTIMATE	$
DESCRIPTION			DESCRIPTION	

KEY IMPLEMENTATION STEPS

1
2
3
4
5
6
7
8
9
10

FUNCTIONAL AREA(S) IMPACTED

INNOVATION GOVERNANCE SECTION

ASSIGNED EVALUATOR		DISPOSITION	☐ Explore ☐ Pass ☐ Hold

DISPOSITION RATIONALE

☐ Yes, proceed with exploration

☐ No, already attempted or in place
☐ No, cost prohibitive
☐ No, not aligned with company mission/vision
☐ Other

Form Importance: Your hope for this form would be for employees to bust the lead off their pencil six times while they're submitting their fellowship ideas because they're so excited that they can't write fast enough! The form needs to embody excitement, but it also needs to drive employees' thought processes. Again, just an idea isn't good enough here. They need to think through how they will go about designing, testing, implementing, and executing a solution within this fellowship. If they have a cool idea but no idea of how to go about looking for a solution or executing it, that is merely a cool idea, not a fellowship. Get enough relevant information to understand the concept and to test their thinking to see if they have something real or not. (Refer back to Chapter 9 for more information on this innovation channel.)

Nuances:

1. The balance between details vs. brevity is key here. You need more details to test their thinking and push them to think through some of the "how." If they can't do it in this form, they are unlikely to be disciplined and experienced enough to do it if the project is approved. But don't make it such that they have to figure out all 100 steps, otherwise they will become frustrated and really aren't testing and stretching their thinking far enough.

2. This form, or "application," can also be considered a weeding tool to ensure you only get full ideas that have had some significant, serious thought behind them. Employees don't need to have the entire project in the bag, but the idea has to be something they have really thought about and can hit the ground running with. The completeness of this form will limit others from submitting ideas that are only half-baked and not ready for prime time.

Crowdsourcing Technology Evaluation Scorecard

replace with
LOGO

CROWDSOURCING TECHNOLOGY CHECKLIST

Input a score of 1-5: **1** = Poor/No, **5** = Excellent/Yes	
QUESTION	SCORE
1. Is this software I install on my hardware, is it a platform as a service, a software as a service or some other type of solution - and how stable is the solution?	3
2. What is the scalability of the solution? Can I manage multiple "campaigns" or innovation challenges?	3
3. Can I manage multiple constituents? (ie – crowdsource from employees, suppliers, customers, general public and do them all together or separately as I desire)	3
4. Do you have a voting feature that can be turned on internally and/or externally? (I've seen solutions where individuals can submit ideas then the population can vote on the ideas they like best – this is great and creates consensus and gives you quick market feedback!)	3
5. Can I build on other's ideas? (leap frog thinking) Some software allows you to "post" a reply to an idea and elaborate on the original idea taking it to another level.	3
6. What is the total cost of ownership - software license/subscription cost, implementation/development cost, maintenance costs, other?	3
7. What is the time and complexity in implementing the solution?	3
8. What is the reporting capability of the core solution and will you have to do customer reporting?	3
9. What is the archiving ability to store, track and recall ideas and related dimensionality of ideas?	3
10. Can I integrate this solution to my email platform so as to manage communications via email?	3
Total Score:	30

Scores = 0 - 19: STOP – validate incapatibility or eliminate this choice
Scores = 21 - 34: Consider customizations, future release features or elimate
Scores = 35+: GO/CONFIRM - technology match appears to have required functionality

Form Importance: This form should help evaluate technology solutions that you might use to help collect, report on, vote on, and evaluate innovative ideas among many constituents. (Refer back to Chapter 10 for more information on this innovation channel.)

Nuances:

1. Do you have various constituent pools (employees, suppliers, customers, coalitions, and so on) that you want to provide innovation thoughts and feedback? How do you want to control and monitor that process?

IVS EXAMPLE REPORTS

At the time of publishing this book, there are several IVS reports available for users of the IVS system and reporting tool. In the following pages, I will describe a handful of those reports as they exist today and provide context on why I see value in the reports as well as recommendations for the actions that can be taken or, at a minimum, the questions that should be asked from these reports. Whether or not you use the IVS system, these reports should give you insights and point to things that you should be looking for in regard to innovation levels and opportunities. (Refer back to Chapter 13 for more information on IVS.)

IVS Summary Scorecard Depicts 16 to 24 individual IVS scores, four category scores, and an overall IVS.

Innovation Value Score®

		Metric IVS	Category IVS	Category Std Dev
Company Size: Company Type: Geo Region: Market Segment: Self Assessed Archetype:	$5M - 100M Non-Profit Canada Manufacturing Customized Solutions Provider			
Customer Value {Custom Solution Provider}	Net Promotor Score	9	4.8	2.7
	Customer Retention	5		
	New Customers	2		
	Strategic Accounts	3		
	CRM Strength	4		
	External Ideation	6		
Growth & Advancement {Product Developer}	New Products over 3 years	2	5.4	3.3
	New Markets over 3 years	9		
	New patents, trademarks, licenses	9		
	Innovation Pipeline	2		
	Brand Awareness	5		
	Speed to Market	5		
Operational Excellence & People {Best Price/Low Cost Leader}	On Time Delivery	7	4.2	2.1
	Employee Retention	4		
	Employee Engagement	4		
	Training dollars per employee	5		
	Quality - Returns	4		
	Supplier value generated	1		
Financial {Proprietary Leader}	Revenue from New Products	6	5.7	2.3
	Capital to Revenue	6		
	Gross Margin Improvement	2		
	Free Cash Flow	4		
	Return on Assets	8		
	Market/Product Exits	7		
Overall Innovation Value Score		**5.0**		
Standard Deviation of all IVS metrics / Category IVS scores		2.5	0.6	

This is a one-page report that summarizes your company's innovation results and indicators, where innovation value is coming from, and the potential areas for improvement.

Questions to Ask:

- Is this the IVS score we predicted? Is it off from our expectations?
- Which areas are different from our assumptions?

- Do our IVS results mirror our strategic intent? (The highest scores are in our strategy archetype.) If not, why are our results off, and what do we need to do to correct this?

- Are the other remaining areas acceptable, or do we need to invest and improve in specific areas?

Potential Action Recommendations:

1. Don't make snap decisions on next steps in relation to the composite score, category scores, or individual scores until you have compared them to other companies. Part of the value of having a common IVS is that you can compare and contrast (i.e., you have context and can improve).

2. Consider sharing this report with other key advisors and consultants to the business (e.g., board advisors, internal auditors, external auditors, consultants you have used in the past, and so on). In sharing the report, ask constituents if they are surprised or find these scores reinforcing what they have come to experience in your business.

IVS Scorecard – Summary + Demographics

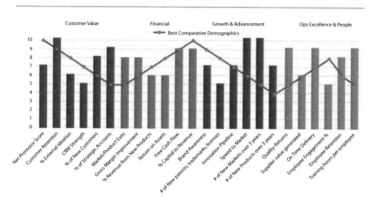

This report has the same summary information as the IVS scores but also includes the demographic information on the companies that have submitted their results to the database. Best Comparative Demographics include company size, industry, geographical area, company type, and business strategy archetype.

Questions to Ask:

- Do these indicators reflect our intended value proposition?
- Would our view change by division, product line, or market segment?
- Is the gap between our business and best comparative demographics acceptable?

Potential Action Recommendations:

1. Consider improvements that you can focus on in relation to improving comparative metrics when compared to similar companies.
2. Review areas where you are excelling to the point that you might want to look beyond your demographics. Set the bar to a higher standard, and compare against others that have best-in-class results in a particular area.

3. Review the targets and goals you need to add to your budgeting process, capital process, operations review processes, and so on so that you can raise the bar on these operating results and drive innovation value to a new level.

IVS Scorecard—Period Comparisons

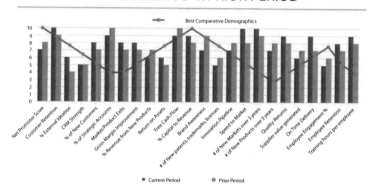

This report shows comparative results of your operating entity period over period. You may have a baseline period listed, quarterly results, or annual results depending on what you have entered into IVS.

Questions to Ask:

- What do we see in these comparative results? Are we moving the bar higher and achieving better results, or are we slipping in areas?

- Do we need to change our strategy, specifically inputs or execution, to get different results?

- What should we expect in the next reporting period? Do we need to adjust our goals?

Potential Action Recommendations:

1. Consider if it would be beneficial to enter some historical information to get year-over-year analysis and results and see what past results have been.

2. Consider the benefit of inputting a forecast or goals period or a scenario into IVS. If you envision where you would like to be from a metric standpoint, you could back into the individual results that would be needed across the business and consider those in your business operating processes, including budgeting, capital management, annual planning, and so on.

IVS Portfolio Balance—Incremental/Distinctive/Breakthrough

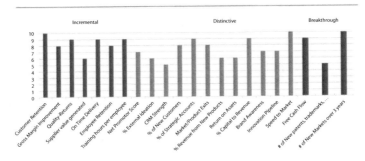

This report shows innovation value created via the portfolio buckets of incremental, distinctive, and breakthrough. While the metrics and buckets may not be perfect, they are a starting point for discussion. They should help you consider whether the resources you're using are in line with the balanced approach that you believe is right for your business at this point in its lifecycle and according to your business strategy.

Questions to Ask:

- Do the IVS metrics in each category reflect current market position and expectations?

- Does the "imbalance" between the three categories reflect our strategy, or are these unintended results?

- Are we properly balanced in short-term payoffs, mid-term improvements, and long-term breakthroughs?

Potential Action Recommendations:

1. Consider resource allocations via your various business processes of budgeting, capital management, and so on. Are you spending your resources in the right proportions to get the results you are striving for in order to achieve your mission and vision, or do you need to rebalance how you are investing and executing?

IVS Portfolio Balance—Lead/Lag

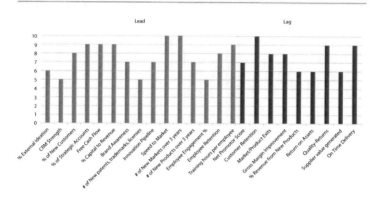

This report shows innovation value created via the portfolio dimensions of leading and lagging indicators. Looking at lead indicators should help you predict lag indicators and overall success of your business strategy if you considered the right causal relationships and execution plans.

Questions to Ask:

- What do these lead indicators tell us about future lag results?
- Are these lag indicators in line with how our business is performing?
- What actions do we need to take to get more foresight and results?
- If we aren't using all 24 IVS metrics, is there one we aren't using that would give us better/additional information for review?

Potential Action Recommendations:

1. Consider if a resource reallocation or rebalancing is required to achieve your mission and vision.

IVS Portfolio Balance—Input/Process/Result

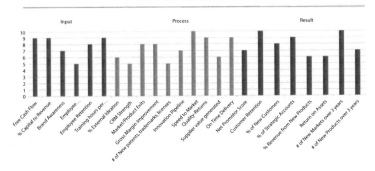

This reports shows innovation value created via the dimensionality of inputs, processes, and results. There are resources or inputs that you use in your business, the execution through processes, and the results you achieve. Looking at metrics in this fashion should help pinpoint areas of improvement to drive more value creation.

Questions to Ask:

- Based on these results, do we need to invest more or reprioritize initiatives to get better results in any of these three groups?

- For low Input scores, do we have an investment issue and need more/different inputs?

- For low Process scores, do we have an execution issue, such as in regard to time, cost, or quality?

- For low Results scores, are they due to inputs or execution? If not, what is driving these results?

Potential Action Recommendations:

1. Consider if a resource reallocation or rebalancing is required to achieve your mission and vision.

2. Consider your business strategy and strategy archetype. If results are lower than expected, find the mismatch between your vision of the business and the results being achieved.

IVS Strategy Map—Innovation Initiatives

IVS Dimensions		Metric	Category	Category	Target	Budget/	
Company Size:	$0 - $4.9M						
Company Type:	For Profit						
Geo Region:	United States						
Market Segment:	Retail	Metric	Category	Category	Target	Budget/	
Strategy Archetype:	Best Price/Low Cost Leader	IVS	IVS	Std Dev	IVS	Invest.	
Customer Value	Net Promotor Score	7					
	Customer Retention	5					
	New Customers	8	4.7	3.1			
(Custom Solution	Strategic Accounts	2					
Provider)	CRM Strength	0					
	External Ideation	6					
Growth &	New Products over 3 years	7					
Advancement	New Markets over 3 years	7					
	New patents, trademarks, licenses	8	5.8	2.9			
	Innovation Pipeline	7					
(Product Leader)	Brand Awareness	6					
	Speed to Market	0					
Operational	On Time Delivery	5					
Excellence & People	Employee Retention	9					
	Employee Engagement	5	4.7	2.9			
(Best Price/Low Cost	Training dollars per employee	4					
Leader)	Quality - Returns	0					
	Supplier value generated	5					
Financial	Revenue from New Products	10					
	Capital to Revenue	7					
	Gross Margin Improvement	8	5.2	4.0			
(Proprietary Leader)	Free Cash Flow	5					
	Return on Assets	0					
	Market/Product Exits	1					
Overall Innovation Value Score		**5.1**					
Standard Deviation of all IVS metrics / Category IVS scores		3.1	0.6				

This report is a repeat of the summary chart, but it prompts the entry and discussion of which IVS metrics to consider as initiatives for improving. Similar to a strategy map, this report would also capture the new IVS target and the specific budget or investment dollars tied to the initiative. This report is ultimately meant to facilitate dialogue and discussion.

Questions to Ask:

- What target levels should we set for improvement, and how do those targets compare against IVS benchmarks, comparable demographics, and best-in-class results?

- What amount should we budget for improvement initiatives?

- What specific strategy (or strategies) will we take to drive an IVS metric to the next level?

Potential Action Recommendations:

1. This seems like an oversimplified report with no new information. The report needs to be completed, however, with the information about your new targets and associated investments to drive more/new results, otherwise you risk achieving more of the same results.

Endnotes

1 Gary Hamel and Nancy Tennant, "The 5 Requirements of a Truly Innovative Company," *Harvard Business Review*, April 27, 2015.

2 Tony Davila, Marc Epstein, and Robert Shelton, *Making Innovation Work: How to Manage It, Measure It, and Profit from It*, Pearson FT Press, 2012.

3 Larry Downes and Paul Nunes, *Big Bang Disruption: Strategy in the Age of Devastating Innovation*, Portfolio, 2014.

4 Marc de Jong, Nathan Marson, and Erik Roth, "The Eight Essentials of Innovation," *McKinsey Quarterly*, April 2015, p. 2.

5 Harvey Wade, Director of Innovation Strategy at Mindjet, as quoted in "Rise of the Chief Innovation Officer—Leading the Way to Transformational Innovation," *Information Age*, April 9, 2014, pp. 1-2.

6 Harvey Wade, Director of Innovation Strategy at Mindjet, as quoted in "Rise of the Chief Innovation Officer—Leading the Way to Transformational Innovation," *Information Age*, April 9, 2014, p. 2.

7 Marc de Jong, Nathan Marson, and Erik Roth, "The Eight Essentials of Innovation," *McKinsey Quarterly*, April 2015, p. 1.

8 Merriam-Webster online dictionary, www.wordcentral.com.

9 www.businessdictionary.com.

10 www.businessdictionary.com.

11 Robert S. Kaplan and David P. Norton, *The Strategy-Focused Organization: How Balanced Scorecard Companies Thrive in the New Business Environment*, Harvard Business School, 2001.

12 Marc de Jong, Nathan Marson, and Erik Roth, "The Eight Essentials of Innovation," *McKinsey Quarterly*, April 2015.

13 Gary Hamel and Nancy Tennant, "The 5 Requirements of a Truly Innovative Company," *Harvard Business Review,* April 2015, p. 7.

14 Patrick J. Stroh, "Business Strategy - Creation, Execution and Monetization," *The Journal of Corporate Accounting & Finance*, May/Jun 2015, pp. 101-105.

15 Bob Dabic, Vistage Leadership Seminar, 2014.

16 IMG and ACCA (Association of Chartered Certified Accountants), *The Changing Role of the CFO*, September 2012.

17 https://en.wikipedia.org/wiki/Galvanization.

18 John Sweeney, *Innovation at the Speed of Laughter*, Aerialist Press, 2007, p. 13.

19 W. Chan Kim and Renee Mauborgne, *Blue Ocean Strategy: How to Create Uncontested Market Space and Make the Competition Irrelevant*, Harvard Business Review Press, 2005, p. 181.

20 Michael Michalko, *Thinkertoys: A Handbook of Creative Thinking Techniques*, Ten Speed Press, 2006, page 24 (adapted).

21 W. Chan Kim and Renee Mauborgne, *Blue Ocean Strategy: How to Create Uncontested Market Space and Make the Competition Irrelevant*, Harvard Business Review Press, 2005, p. 162

22 APQC, *Successfully Embedding Innovation*, 2010, p. 2.

23 APQC, *Open Innovation: Enhancing Idea Generation Through Collaboration*, 2013, p. 2.

24 APQC, *Successfully Embedding Innovation*, 2010, p. 2.

25 Clay Christensen, "Finding an Ideal Metric for Innovation," *Inc.*, June 2014.

26 Robert S. Kaplan and David P. Norton, *Strategy Maps: Converting Intangible Assets into Tangible Outcomes*, Harvard Business Review Press, 2004.

27 APQC, *Innovating On Your Own Terms*, 2007, p. 2.

Recommended Reading

For some background on innovation, and specifically in relation to innovation governance, I suggest you take a look at the Kaplan and Norton books as some foundational baseline and research support for what this book covered on innovation itself and the leadership and governance needed around innovation. Kaplan and Norton's Balanced Scorecard Management System has three levels that can be mapped to the base elements of the Innovation Elixir:

1. *An integrated management system*

2. *A philosophy of management*

3. *An economic model of value creation*

Consider the following mapping:

A Philosophy of Management □→ *Galvanizing*

An Integrated Management System → *Enabling*

An Economic Model of Value Creation → *Measuring*

Therefore, as you consider at each of these three elements, you may find value in looking back at some of these Kaplan and Norton works that provide foundation and research in each of the key areas:

Read *The Execution Premium* and *Alignment* for more on an integrated management system. *The Strategy-Focused Organization* addresses a philosophy of management. And *The Balanced Scorecard and Strategy Maps* cover an economic model of value creation.

CORE INNOVATION THOUGHT LEADERSHIP

In addition to the works of Kaplan and Norton in baseline strategy and execution, one name that often comes up in conversations about innovation is Clay Christensen. His book, *The Innovator's Dilemma*, formed a baseline for thought leadership around disruptive innovation and what causes great firms to succeed and fail. Although it was written in 1997, it still has relevance and significance today. There are many cases, points, and reference points I could make to this body of work, but I'd specifically highlight two areas of work that directly pertain to the discussion of innovation governance and execution.

I. *"Three classes of factors affect what an organization can and cannot do: its resources, its processes and its values."* Christensen was discussing an organization's capabilities framework and what needs to be in place. If you think about galvanizing, enabling, and measuring—it is similar to an extent.

Galvanizing equals Values—ensuring your organization is ready to execute and understands the value and significance. The Innovation Elixir begins with this element first because the organization needs to be galvanized or the rest of the process is for naught.

Enabling equals Processes—talking about how resources (people, time, money) will be transformed to create value via new products and services of greater worth. Process is key—and finding the right processes at the right level so your culture accepts and thrives is truly part of the Innovation Elixir.

The third class of factors is where Christensen differs from the Innovation Elixir. His third factor is Resources, which is part of the Enabling element. The third element of the Innovation Elixir, on the other hand, is Measuring. It is when we measure and discuss value creation that we will do a better job of assigning resources and creating additional value. As you saw, the work only begins with the actual measurement. That's followed by taking actions to drive improvement—otherwise, why did you take the time to measure in the first place?

II. Christensen offers seven Innovator's Dilemmas in his book. I'd like to address and discuss their specific relevance here.

1. *"The pace of progress that markets demand or can absorb may be different from the progress offered by technology."* Being too early or late to the market with your idea is still relevant today, and this dilemma needs to get fleshed out via the measuring element. But it also needs your "gut feel" (instincts), experience, and leadership capability.

2. *"Managing innovation mirrors the resource allocation process: Innovation proposals that get the funding and manpower they require may succeed; those given lower priority, whether formally or de facto, will starve for lack of resources and have little chance of success."* I couldn't agree more! This is why innovation governance is needed. Innovation efforts, projects, and ideas need to be handled via regular business processes. The enabling channels that are described in Chapters 6–10 need to be tied into existing business processes for resource allocation, decision making, and monitoring. *Don't* make innovation governance a *separate* exercise.

3. *"Just as there is a resource allocation side to every innovation problem, matching the market to the technology is another."* Christensen is talking here about disruptive innovation. When something is truly disruptive, there isn't a market or demand for it. By definition, it is disrupting something that exists. One major benefit we have today vs. when this book was written is the advent of crowdsourcing as a way of testing the marketplace (see Chapter 10). Yes, you still need to match the market to your new innovation, but you can more easily test the market via crowdsourcing capabilities. If you are not taking advantage of this easy, fast, and effective way of assessing market potential, you may be seriously missing out!

4. *"The capabilities of most organizations are far more specialized and context-specific than most managers are inclined to believe."* This dilemma addresses the status quo for existing business processes and cycles and how good companies are good at execution and not as good at making changes. In the galvanizing element, you will be fighting the very forces that are making you successful, so you have to find a way to look at products and processes differently—for different customers, markets, and utilization without jeopardy to what you are doing today. You need to set the right context and ready the organization for select experimentation.

5. *"In many instances, the information required to make large and decisive investments in the face of disruptive technology simply does not exist."* Again, if the innovation is truly disruptive, there should be little if any market data because you are doing something totally different. This is the very reason that Chapter 5 talks about incremental, distinctive, and breakthrough innovations. Breakthrough is akin to disruptive innovation. And if you are singularly focused on breakthrough innovations, you may be unnecessarily betting the farm on products/services/markets that may or may not materialize.

6. *"It is not wise to adopt a blanket technology strategy to be always a leader or always a follower."* Balance, balance, balance. In some things, you will take a leadership position, in others you will follow. This needs to be monitored in the measurement element. It is when you are looking at your total portfolio, your total value proposition that you decide where to place big bets on market leadership positions and where to take less risk. This should be at the heart of good innovation governance and overall strategic leadership and execution.

7. *"There are powerful barriers to entry and mobility that differ significantly from the types defined and historically focused on by*

economists." This dilemma is only exacerbated by the speed of change, globalization, and technology today. Size and economies of scale used to be critical, but speed, the ability to change, and nimbleness are equally, if not more, important in today's landscape. Globalization and distribution of products, services, and information via the Internet has created a great equalizer between large and small companies. Speed and barriers to entry should be considered in all of the innovation channels and measurement.

StrengthsFinder

At least four million people are familiar with the book and findings of *StrengthsFinder*. The first printing and research came out in 2007. You may also be familiar with the related work, *First Break All the Rules*. This is one of my favorite business books and something to put on your reading pile if you haven't already. In one statement: These works are about *individuals recognizing and capitalizing on their strengths vs. focusing on fixing their perceived weaknesses.* When you think about the performance review process at most companies and talking to employee's about "how to fix their weaknesses," it's quite arbitrary and, in my mind (and supported by the *StrengthsFinder* research), backwards. Your time is better spent focusing on employees' strengths and finding ways to align their strengths and personal goals with your business's needs and goals rather than looking for ways to "fix" their weaknesses. Makes sense to me!

Big Bang Disruption

Authors Paul Lunes and Larry Downes do an excellent job of laying out what innovation looked like circa 2014. They outline three distinct eras of innovation and provide some historical strategy and innovation context that is important to better understand our challenges of today:

1. *Conventional wisdom held that new markets were created from the top down. Michael Porter of Harvard Business School outlined innovating along one of three "generic" strategies, but all top down.*

   a. *Differentiate their market offerings with special features and sell at a premium.*

   b. *Optimized production efficiencies and sell at a lower price.*

   c. *A variation on a. and b. but focusing on serving just one segment of the market extremely well.*

2. *Clay Christensen challenged the top-down view of innovation and persuaded that disruptive innovators work from the bottom up. His*

work on disruptive innovation also focused on disruptive technologies and their value over time—from early adoption and value to commercialization.

3. *The third stage of strategic thinking on innovation comes from W. Chan Kim and Renee Maubornge via* Blue Ocean Strategy. *This work focuses on disrupters that innovate around new and unmet needs in existing, even mature, categories coming at them from more or less "sideways."*

Lunes and Downes then argue that we are now in the "fourth stage" of innovation, the era of "Big Bang Disruption." They describe innovation not as disruptive innovation, but as "devastating innovation"! This book is worth a read. It may scare the hell out of you as a leader and keep you up at night as you consider new competitors coming at you from all angles and sources, entering existing markets in swift, deft moves, but it may also make you think just a bit differently on market disruption.

Blue Ocean Strategy

Lunes and Downes mention the last book on my recommended reading list: *Blue Ocean Strategy* by W. Chan Kim and Renee Maubornge. In it, Kim and Maubornge write, *"Chief executives should instead use value and innovation as the important parameters for managing their portfolio of business. They should use innovation because without it companies are struck in the trap of competitive improvements. They should use value because innovation ideas will be profitable only if they are linked to what buyers are willing to pay for."* Innovation has to be about value creation! You need a certain level of innovation activity to get results, but don't confuse activity with results. At the end of the day, innovation is valuable if it creates value for your customers or members. While chief executives should use innovation as a parameter, how are they measuring innovation value? Innovation measurement has been a confusing, convoluted topic, and that is why I dug into it.

Acknowledgments

I would like to thank those who contributed to the success of this book and our larger innovation body of work. I hope this innovation "how to" guide and measurement and management system will aid in your discovery of more and better ways to innovate and drive value in your businesses!

Next, a few well-deserved thank-yous. I'd like to thank IMA® (Institute of Management Accountants) for approaching me about writing this book on innovation and to make a meaningful contribution to the advancement of our profession and the market as a whole. I've been a CMA® since 1992 — IMA is an important organization to me, and I'm happy we've been able to work together on this initiative to drive value to our members and our profession.

I'd like to thank Palladium, a leader in balanced scorecarding and strategy execution consulting. The support and inputs from a variety of individuals in their organization has been invaluable.

I'd like to thank the American Productivity and Quality Center (APQC). APQC is a thought leader in the benchmarking community and have been supportive in working with me on this endeavor, and I've been happy to work with them.

I'd also like to thank the triad of SalesForce; Strategic Growth, the technology developer of SalesForce; and Drawloop, the reporting partner within SalesForce. All three of these organizations provided value, creativity, troubleshooting, and ultimately delivered the Innovation Value Score® (IVS) platform that I envisioned. I appreciate the support, validation, fierce conversations, and thought leadership from all these organizations.

I'd also like to call out some specific individuals that grabbed a laboring oar in getting this work to the finish line. Thanks to the team at IMA, led by Jeff Thomson, an intelligent businessman, a savvy leader, and a friend. Thank you, Jeff, for our many conversations at all hours of day and night, which ultimately led to where we are today in driving value in our profession. Thanks also to Kip Krumwiede, who led the research and analysis of the results, and to many others at IMA who helped with various vetting and reviews, communications, and other important supporting work.

Thanks to the individuals at Palladium, led by John McClellan, a gentleman who brings a great deal to the business world and is always thinking of value creation for organizations. Thanks to Ian Pallister and Karen

DiMartino and all others at Palladium who reviewed, contributed, analyzed, challenged, and supported this book and its supporting concepts and systems. This group is talented and motivated, and I'm pleased to have had the opportunity to work with them and look forward to continuing to do so.

I'd next like to thank the technology team of Mike Teegan, Bonnie Weinandt, Len Doland, and Cory Bevilacqua, who collaborated together to stand up the platform as it was envisioned and allowed us to conduct the IVS pilot research. Thanks for working your associated "punch lists" and making this innovation solution provide meaningful insights with a friendly experience.

Thank you to Jay Highum of Action Graphic Design and Bonnie Weinandt of Unlimited Support, the creative designers and technology developers behind all of the logos, branding, websites, book jacket, etc. They are both very talented and action-oriented people—I couldn't have asked for better creative and implementation masters.

A special thank you to Dr. Robert Kaplan, Harvard professor and co-creator of the Balanced Scorecard and author of a plethora of books. Bob's early feedback in how we were using a balanced scorecard framework and his insights from years of consulting and implementing scorecards at companies were invaluable. The initial IVS scorecard and measurement system used in the pilot and now in full production is more of a version 3.0 or 4.0 as we leapfrogged what could have been earlier versions simply by talking with Bob and listening to his feedback and reactions to the methodology.

Lastly, a special thank you to my family and friends. To my wife and kids who continuously listen to my stories, read my writing, offer thoughts on creative, and put up with my hours and travel. Thank you for supporting me. To extended family and friends, who also listen to my updates and stories and offer their thoughts—thank you!

To anyone I may have mistakenly omitted, please accept my apologies. There is no shortage of people whom I respect, seek the counsel of, and whose ears I bend from time to time—thank you!

About the Author

Patrick is president of Mercury Business Advisors, which provides management advisory services in business strategy, innovation, product development, and turnaround situations, and is also author of *Business Strategy: Plan, Execute, Win!* He is on the board of directors for IMA® (Institute of Management Accountants), which serves more than 75,000 accountants and financial professionals in 140 countries, and also for Vail Place, a Minneapolis-based agency supporting those with mental illness. He was appointed in 2014 to serve on the COSO Advisory Board to review the update of the 2004 COSO Enterprise Risk Framework. Prior to consulting, he most recently held positions within UnitedHealth Group, including chief strategy & innovation officer, client experience officer, president consumer health products, and senior vice president of business strategy. Patrick also writes a column entitled Innovation Elixir® for the American City Business Journals covering 43 metro markets across the U.S., is an active member of the Prior Lake Rotary Club, and is a classically trained chef having studied at Le Cordon Bleu in Minneapolis.

978-0-9967293-07-MAN